ANTHONY BURGESS

Modern Critical Views

These and other titles in preparation

Modern Critical Views

ANTHONY BURGESS

Edited and with an introduction by
Harold Bloom
Sterling Professor of the Humanities
Yale University

CHELSEA HOUSE PUBLISHERS ◊ 1987
New York ◊ New Haven ◊ Philadelphia

Library of Congress Cataloging-in-Publication Data

Anthony Burgess.

  (Modern critical views)
  Bibliography: p.
  Includes index.
  1. Burgess, Anthony, 1917-   —Criticism and
interpretation. I. Bloom, Harold. II. Series.
PR6052.U638Z54 1987   823'.914 86–24459
ISBN 0-87754-676-2 (alk. paper)

Contents

Editor's Note

This book gathers together what I judge to be a representative selection of the best criticism available upon the novels of Anthony Burgess. I am grateful for David Parker's devoted work as a researcher for this volume.

After my introduction, which centers upon Burgess's relationship to Joyce, particularly in the Enderby novels and *Nothing Like the Sun,* the critical essays are reprinted here in the chronological order of their original publication. The sequence begins with Christopher Ricks, who offers an overview of Burgess's early novels and holds out the hope that Burgess might yet do better. In another early overview, William H. Pritchard takes issue with Ricks and gives a more generous estimate.

Charles G. Hoffmann and A. C. Hoffmann explore the first two Enderby novels, finding in Enderby a dark laughter that is a saving grace in a thoroughly bad time. *A Clockwork Orange* and *The Wanting Seed,* Burgess's two visions of dystopia, are examined by Robert K. Morris, who finds in them parables of freedom despoiled. John J. Stinson, analyzing Burgess as a contemporary Manichee, uncovers the fundamental dualism present in all of the novels. The double vision of Burgess, clearly related to this Manichean dualism, is analyzed by Jean E. Kennard as a formidable instance of the post-Existential dilemma.

A Clockwork Orange, doubtless Burgess's best known book though clearly not one of his best, is seen by Esther Petix as an accurate prophecy of increasingly menacing social realities. Robert Martin Adams, an eminent critic of Joyce, also considers *A Clockwork Orange* and *Tremor of Intent* in the context of Joyce's influence upon Burgess.

In the first of his two critical pieces here, Geoffrey Aggeler gives us an extensive overview of Burgess's theological stance as a writer. Invoking Shelley, Timothy R. Lucas establishes what might be called Burgess's prevalent metaphor of Prometheanism and is supplemented by Aggeler's analysis of the figure of Faust in Burgess's *Earthly Powers*. Finally,

Walter Kerr takes us full circle back to the concerns of my introduction, as he reviews *Enderby's Dark Lady* and expresses the welcome of "all those Burgess fans who simply cannot conceive of a world without Enderby."

Introduction

I

Anthony Burgess has the same relationship to James Joyce that Samuel Beckett has; dangerous as this comparison is (and Burgess has too much sense to welcome it), we can utilize it to define the nature and limits of Burgess's considerable achievement as a novelist and man-of-letters. Though Burgess has no *Murphy* (Beckett's genial, early comic masterpiece) he has the marvelous Enderby saga (*Inside Mr. Enderby; Enderby Outside; The Clockwork Testament; or, Enderby's End; Enderby's Dark Lady; or, No End to Enderby*) and the even grander *Nothing Like the Sun: A Story of Shakespeare's Love-life.* Whether writing about Enderby (a vision of Burgess himself as uncompromising poet) or Shakespeare, Burgess truly writes about Joyce's Poldy Bloom, and so about Joyce himself.

Murphy is as much an interpretation of *Ulysses* as the Enderby cycle or *Nothing Like the Sun* is, but *Murphy* already manifests a revisionary swerve away from the master, "a *clinamen* to the ideal," as Coleridge once called it. Beckett revised Joyce more cunningly still in *Watt* and the great trilogy of *Molloy, Malone Dies, and The Unnamable*, and that sly misprision of the only twentieth-century novelist to rival Proust is the foundation of Beckett's eminence as the strongest living writer in English or French today. Burgess has a more limited ambition, and enters into no *agon* with Joyce, however loving. Towards Joyce, he is the thankful receiver or good son, a humanly heartening stance but perhaps also one that balks the full freedom of creation.

Reviewing a biography of Beckett, Burgess shrewdly caught the subtle relationship between Joyce and Beckett, strong father and strong, so necessarily cast-out, son:

Beckett's books and plays posit a Cartesian division between

1

mind and body. (His first published work, the poem *Whoroscope*, is a kind of gorblimied life of Descartes.) Those heroes and heroines on their last, or nonexistent, legs, assert a powerful identity in spite of the wreck of the flesh. It is the kind of work one might expect from a lifelong invalid. His biography shows that Beckett was always an athlete, a well-coordinated car driver and motorbike rider who could smash the machine but emerge whole, an excellent swimmer and fine cricketer — the only Nobel Prizeman to be mentioned in *Wisden*. His body has always been spare and tough, able to take any amount of punishment from drink and cigarettes. But one notes a kind of self-flagellancy. A worshipper of Joyce, he took to pretending he had Joyce's feet, which were small and dainty and pleased their owner: he crippled himself with unsuitable shoes. But the body's main pains, and its Oblomov lethargy, seem to have most to do with Beckett's complicated relationship with his mother. . . .

It is somewhat eery to find that the ancient *faible* of Lucia Joyce continued, long after her father's death and the end of Ellmann's record. Time stopped for her, and Beckett remained the young hawklike man who shared the master's silences and, after his rejection of the demented girl's advances, was icily told not to call again. Beckett's devotion to Joyce continues, and his own artistic perfectionism, in the study and theatre alike, is its best expression. He works himself and his actors to the limit. The account of Billie Whitelaw's creative ordeal with him is one of the most remarkable chapters of this book.

The Muse his mother reclaims Beckett from Joyce here in the first paragraph, moving us from the cheerful, curious, active Poldy to the sublimely lethargic Murphy, and all the nearly inanimate Beckett protagonists who came after him. Icily rejected after refusing Lucia's schizophrenic advances, Beckett is seen by Burgess as carrying the father's aesthetic perfectionism to new limits. This is legitimate enough, but chooses to evade the dwindling of Joyce's idiom in Beckett, from its palpable presence in *Murphy* to its total absence in the later, astonishingly laconic narratives, if narratives they be.

Contrast Burgess on his "favorite novel," *Ulysses:*

And yet it is not quite a novel. I have lived long enough with *Ulysses* to be fully aware of its faults, and its major fault is that it evades the excruciating problem that most novelists set themselves: how, without blatant contrivance, to show character in the process of change, so that the reader, saying goodbye to Mr X or Miss Y, realizes that these are not quite the people he met at the beginning. There is, in every non-Joycean novel, a psychological watershed hardly discernible to the reader; without the imposition of a journey to this watershed fictional character can hardly be said to exist. In *Ulysses,* whose action covers less than twenty-four hours, there is no time for change. Indeed, nothing happens of sufficient gravity to induce change. The ordinary man Bloom meets the extraordinary youth Stephen and then says a goodnight which is probably a goodbye. Molly Bloom dreams of Stephen as a kind of messianic son-lover. Whatever happens in the novel, it does not happen today. It ends on the brink of tomorrow, when something may possibly happen, but tomorrow never comes. That is the novel's major fault.

It is a fault so massive that it can only be compensated for by exceptional virtues, and these virtues I have already hinted at — the epic vitality of the scheme, the candour of the presentation of human life as it really is, the awe-inspiring virtuosity of the language. Add to these the comprehensiveness of the urban vision it provides. When we visit Dublin we carry that vision with us; it is more real than the flesh-and-blood or stone- and-mortar reality. We cannot, I suppose, finally judge *Ulysses* as a work of fiction at all. It is a kind of magical codex, of the same order as Dante's *Divine Comedy* (in which hell, heaven and purgatory go on for ever and nothing changes). But, in the practical terms in which writers are forced to think, it is a terrible literary challenge. To call it my favourite novel is, I see, shame-fully inept. It is the work I have to measure myself hopelessly against each time I sit down to write fiction.

Has Burgess found, in the manner of the strong novelist, the fault that is not there in his precursor's masterwork? I suspect that he is asking Joyce to be Shakespeare, whose greatest originality came in representing how his characters changed through the process of listening to what they themselves had said. Burgess's Shakespeare is overtly Joyce's Shakespeare, so that *Nothing Like the Sun* is not less overtly Joycean than is the Enderby cycle. Joyce's own originality, even as a parodist, is rightly celebrated as being extraordinary. Even as Proust was found by his true precursor in the not-very-novelistic Ruskin (who nevertheless fused with Flaubert in the influence process), so Joyce owed less to Flaubert than he did to Shakespeare. *Ulysses* is not so much an interpretation of Homer, or even of Dante, as it is of *Hamlet*.

Joyce's *Hamlet* is an act of strong misreading, in which the poetic father, Shakespeare, is diminished so that the vital son, Joyce, can mature. This creation by interpretation, marked by zest, verve, saturnine wit, must be the most striking account of *Hamlet* ever given to us. Shakespeare is not Hamlet, but the ghost of Hamlet's father, a role that he actually played on stage (doubling as the Player King), according to tradition. Hamlet is Stephen, or the portrait of the artist as a young man. Poor Shakespeare has been cuckolded not just by one brother, as Hamlet senior was by Claudius, but by two, both of whom have had their way with Anne Hathaway. If this were not sexual defeat enough, Shakespeare in addition has lost the dark lady of the sonnets, presumably to an honorary third brother, or best friend. Stephen's theory proposes that Shakespeare's dead son, Hamnet, enters the play as Hamlet, to recover his father's honor through an act of revenge. This resurrected son of Shakespeare does not lust after Anne Hathaway, or Gertrude, and can be regarded as a proleptic representation of Anthony Burgess, who did not refuse the gift.

In the Circe episode of *Ulysses,* Poldy and Stephen, each a representative of Shakespeare / Joyce, stare into a mirror and confront a transmogrified Shakespeare, beardless and "rigid in facial paralysis." Joyce is a beardless Shakespeare, lacking the Bard's virility, and frozen-faced where the precursor is mobile and expressive. Again, Burgess took the hint, even if he did not quite join in Joyce's ironic self-judgment. Stephen cites the Sabellian heresy, which holds that the Father was Himself His Own Son, a view that makes Shakespeare into Joyce, and Joyce into Burgess. Burgess, a good Freudian (Joyce evaded Freud, properly), believes rather that the Son was Himself His Own Father, a faith that makes Joyce into Shakespeare, and Burgess, rather wistfully, almost into Joyce.

II

Burgess, by need and conviction, exuberantly exemplifies the Johnsonian apothegm that only a blockhead would write for anything except money. The consequence is an immense output, not much of which bears rereading. His most famous novel, *A Clockwork Orange* (1962), owes its notoriety more to Stanley Kubrick's film version than to its own text, and his overtly religious narratives (the book-length poem *Moses* and such excursions as *Man of Nazareth*) are interesting primarily as instances of the writer's Manichean dualism, which has replaced Burgess's lapsed Catholicism. But two of the novels I reread annually: *Inside Mr. Enderby* (1963) and *Nothing Like the Sun* (1964). Enderby triumphantly returned in *Enderby Outside* (1968), only to be killed off by his ungrateful creator in *The Clockwork Testament; or, Enderby's End* (1975), which provoked a fierce outcry by devoted Enderbyans, among whom I number myself. In response to our laments and protests, Burgess gave us *Enderby's Dark Lady; or, No End to Enderby*, a superb amalgam of *Inside Mr. Enderby* and *Nothing Like the Sun*. It is now to be hoped that Enderby, and "William Shakespeare," will last as long as Burgess does, may it be forever.

Inside Mr. Enderby is one of my own candidates for the most undervalued English novel of our era, since the raffish narrative clearly has immortality in it. Enderby himself is at once Leopold Bloom, James Joyce, William Shakespeare, and Anthony Burgess, which is merely outrageous, and totally successful. As a true poet, Enderby is also Samuel Johnson, Jonathan Swift, John Keats, Walt Whitman, and perhaps such modern roisterers as Dylan Thomas and Brendan Behan, which only means that Enderby is a universal representation of the fate of the poet in a world necessarily and simultaneously too good for him and not quite good enoughfor anyone of imagination.

Everything that is conceivable happens to Enderby, or perhaps rather Enderby is what happens to everyone else in his world. Like Poldy, Enderby is the complete man or the compassionate man, except that Poldy is a Jewish respecter of learning and art and a bit of an artist himself, but no poet, which is Stephen's vocation — and Enderby's. Enderby is also obsessed by guilt, quite unmerited, whereas Poldy is beyond guilt, being a kind of Messiah, a text that is an answer, though obscure. The Enderby books, never obscure, refuse all answers. Amidst so much tawdry splendor, which never ceases to proliferate, I cite as a favorite passage the sublime moment when Enderby graciously declines the Goodby gold medal for poetry at a luncheon in London, a paradigm of all the literary luncheons where, like Enderby, the critic Bloom has gotten quite drunk:

> "And it is for this reason that it gives me pleasure to bestow on our fellow singing-bird here, er er Enderby, the Goodby gold medal." Enderby rose to applause loud enough to drown three cracking intestinal reports. "And a cheque," said Sir George, with nostalgia of poet's poverty, "that is very very small but, one trusts, will stave off pangs for a month or two." Enderby took his trophies, shook hands, simpered, then sat down again.

"Speech," said somebody. Enderby rose again, with a more subdued report, then realised that he was unsure of the exordial protocol. Did he say, "Mr. Chairman"? Was there a chairman? If Sir George was the chairman should he say something other than "Mr. Chairman"? Should he just say, "Sir George, ladies and gentlemen"? But, he noticed, there seemed to be somebody with a chain of office gleaming on his chest, hovering in the dusk, a mayor or lord mayor. What should he say—"Your Worship"? In time he saw that this was some sort of menial in charge of wine. Holding in wind, a nervously smiling Aeolus, Enderby said, loud and clear:

"St George." There was a new stir of tittering. "And the dragon," Enderby now had to add. "A British cymbal," he continued, seeing with horror that orthographical howler in a sort of neon lights before him. "A cymbal that tinkles in unsound brass if we are without clarity." There were appreciative easings of buttocks and shoulders: Enderby was going to make it brief and humorous. Desperately Enderby said, "As most of us are or are not, as the case may be. Myself included." Sir George, he saw, was throwing up wide face-holes at him, as though he, Enderby, were on a girder above the street. "Clarity," said Enderby, almost in tears, "is red wine for yodellers. And so," he gaped aghast at himself, "I am overjoyed to hand back this cheque to St George for charitable disposal. The gold medal he knows what he can do with." He could have died with shock and embarrassment at what he was saying; he was hurled on to the end in killing momentum, however. "Dross of the workaday world," he said "as our fellow-singer Goodby so adequately disproves. And so," he said, back in the Army giving a talk on the British Way and Purpose, "we look forward to a time when the world shall be free of the shadow of oppression, the iron heel with its swastika spur no longer grinding into the face of supine freedom, democracy a reality, a fair day's pay for a fair day's work, adequate health services and a bit of peace hovering dovelike in the declining days of the aged. And in that belief and aspiration we move forward." He found that he could not stop. "Forward," he insisted, "to a time when the world shall be free of the shadow of oppression." Sir George had risen and was tottering out. "A fair day's work," said Enderby feebly, "for a fair day's pay. Fair play for all," he mumbled doubtfully. Sir George had gone. "And thereto," ended Enderby wretchedly,

"I plight thee my truth."

The model for Enderby's peroration is Poldy's proclamations of the New Bloomusalem in the Nova Hibernia of the future, in the Nighttown episode of *Ulysses*, except that Poldy, as always, is sober, while Enderby, as always, is drunk. In some ways Enderby combines the traits of a Buck Mulligan emptied out of all malice, with the lovable amiability of Poldy, gentlest of all representations in fiction. This may be too much of a problem in depiction for Burgess and may account for the gradual evolution of Enderby away from Poldy and Joyce and towards Burgess's "William Shakespeare," as the cycle takes its labyrinthine pratfalls on to *Enderby's Dark Lady*. What is certain is that no single Enderby book is quite as effective as *Nothing Like the Sun*, not even *Inside Mr. Enderby*, though finally I might set that highest in the Burgess canon. For sustained command of language, Shakespearean and Joycean, *Nothing Like the Sun* is Burgess's most accomplished performance, as here in a vision of Elizabethan London as the demonic context of the great love affair between Shakespeare and the dark lady of the *Sonnets:*

> London, the defiled city, became a sweet bower for their lover's wandering, even in the August heat. The kites that hovered or, perched, picked at the flesh of traitors' skulls became good cleansing birds, bright of eye and feather, part of the bestiary of myth that enthralled them as they made it. The torn and screaming bears and dogs and apes in the pits of Paris Garden were martyrs who rose at once into gold heraldic zoomorphs to support the scutcheon of their static and sempiternal love. The wretches that lolled in chains on the lapping edges of the Thames, third tide washed over, noseless, lipless, eye-eaten, joined the swinging hanged at Tyburn and the rotting in the jails to be made heroes of a classical hell that, turned into music by Vergil, was sweet and pretty schoolday innocence. But it was she who shook her head often in sadness, smiling beneath her diaphanous veil as they took the evening air in passion's convalescence, saying that autumn would soon be on them, that love's fire burned flesh and then itself—out, gone for ever.

This is the only apocalypse acceptable to Burgess, heroic vitalist and celebrator of the things of this world: "Love's fire burned flesh and then itself—out, gone for ever." That is a burden hardly unique to Burgess, and the accent remains Joycean, yet the music of this mortality verges upon being Burgess's alone.

CHRISTOPHER RICKS

The Epicene

Ten novels since 1956 — that is the fact about Anthony Burgess. Some of his well-wishers think it looks irresponsible, but surely it is his fertility which makes one hopeful of a first-rate comic novel. He hasn't yet written it; no single one of his books focuses all the best in his writing. No doubt he has been embarrassed by the gratifying words of reviewers; to deserve them all, he would have to be a much better novelist than Dickens. His prodigality is in a sense undiscriminating, a fact which comes out glumly in his new British Council pamphlet, *The Novel Today*. He does his best to protect himself against the suspicion that such pamphlets have the casually inflated hospitality of the party that Don Juan went to ("Also the 80 greatest living poets"), so he borrows a look of rigour: "If the novel is not to be debased, we must practise an almost cruel stringency of judgement." But far from being stringent, he even has to fall back upon "may yet emerge as." The pamphlet is merely jolly. The difference in liveliness between the pamphlet and the novels would define his kind of creative talent.

His reputation, like Waugh's and Greene's, seems to be of the sort that is bound to zoom and plunge. Since it is high now he is in his mid-forties (posh reviewer, interviewed on TV and radio, British Councillor), one must resist the envious urge to take a hand in turning fortune's wheel about. Anyway *Honey for the Bears* is one of his best books, and an oddly subversive one both politically and sexually. Paul Hussey is an antique

---

From *The New Statesman* 65, no. 1673 (April 5, 1963). © 1963 by The Statesman and Nation Publishing Co.

dealer from Sussex, on a trip to Leningrad with his American wife Belinda. Business rather than pleasure, since they are smuggling in a lot of drilon dresses; they plan to make a thousand pounds, for the benefit of a friend who is a widow. Russia turns out to be disconcertingly like America (even in its RC-versy godliness), so that politically the book is about a Third Force that will combine and outdo them. Sexually it is about the same thing, since Paul and Belinda find out, or at last admit, that they are homosexual, though that hasn't stopped them from being heterosexual as well.

Does this seem old hat rather than subversion? I don't think so, and one might ask where the Tweedledum and Tweedledee feeling about Russia and America has yet found expression in a novel. Likewise, novels tend to be *either/or* about sex, dealing in the notion that so-and-so is *a* homosexual rather than homosexual, that he or she will prove to be *really* one or the other despite sad attempts at the wrong one. In fact the novelty of the book doesn't lie exactly there, but in its invincibly comic treatment of these two ideas of a Third Force. Instead of lordly moral claims to political sainthood, there is the idea that life won't be any more dangerous and is very likely to be more fun. And instead of the transcendental mysticism of Mr G. Wilson Knight's paean to bisexuality — "the seraphic intuition" of Byron, Lawrence and Christ — there is the idea that being able to enjoy both is to find more to enjoy and so to add to the public stock of harmless pleasure. That homosexuality is not wicked, not ethereally spiritual, not necessarily the source of anxiety or agony, not incompatible with other things, but a rather pleasant virtuosity — if this is not subversive, what would be? Paul and Belinda don't terribly mind when they find out about themselves. "All things contain their opposite," Paul keeps reflecting, but this is the first time that Mr Burgess has applied this to sexuality; in his first novel it was only political, the merry pre-war Marxist version of "Green Grow the Rushes, Oh":

> Two, two, the opposites
> Interpenetrating though...

Mr Burgess has all the current awareness of how hard it is to pin anything on a novelist. When someone suggested that Patrick Standish in *Take a Girl Like You* is nasty like his creator, Kingsley Amis wrote a sharp note saying that Standish was a character in a book — as if the question of whether an author connived could be settled simply by his saying he didn't. (In fact, Standish seems to me unswervingly criticized, but that needs to be demonstrated and not just pronounced.) So Mr Burgess might complain of misrepresentation, in which case it would be enough to claim that his novel is a humanely funny discussion of an unusual point of view. The jokes are not always good, but a pointed one leaps from the way in which the Russians transliterate G and H; Paul Hussey becomes Pavel Gussey (no longer a shameful Hussey?), and more importantly homosexuality becomes gomosexuality—an excellent device for stripping it of spirituality, guilt, introversion.

The author's imagination, too, is released. One of the rare moments when Salinger's Bluddy Glass is distinguishable from his brother Buddy Gass comes when Buddy maintains that

> there is an enormous amount of the androgynous in any all-or-nothing prose writer, or even a would-be one. I think that if he titters at male writers who wear invisible skirts he does so at his eternal peril.

This is certainly a genuine part of what Mr Burgess is trying to say: in his pamphlet he claims that Angus Wilson's distinctive contribution to the novel has been "taking seriously the homosexual sensibility." Taking it comically might be his own praise, and this does not mean sneeringly. Throughout the novels he has apparently been trying to make up his mind about the epicene, and in the first one *(Time for a Tiger)* his prose took on a delighted and very uncensorious lilt as it observed androgynous Ibrahim: "Undulating through the market, who so gay as Ibrahim?" No guilt for Ibrahim. The futurist fable, *The Wanting Seed,* begins with a world in which overpopulation has made homosexuality socially most desirable, so that the posters say "It's Sapiens to be Homo" and "Love Your Fellow-Men." Such a situation is thought to be unfortunate because of the public vindictiveness about heterosexuality, but even here there is a notable absence of disgust. And when heterosexuality resumes its baby-bringing reign, we find that we just have King Stork.

All this has been about the ideas of the book, shocking in the same genial way as Fielding (both of them mildly suggesting that many kinds of sexual immorality don't in fact much matter). But the novel is inventive and gay as well. For me a clear advantage which it has over some of the earlier ones is that it abandons horror comedy, the mingling of black realistic violence and comic lightness. True, at one point a Russian policeman punches Paul, but then the policeman is at once genuinely contrite, and the novel as a whole has a straightforward and old-fashioned comic decorum. Many of the previous ones seem spoiled by their black comedy. Even if one accepts that in theory there is no reason why the two shouldn't mingle, it does seem that in practise it is a very great deal harder to do than one would guess from the sheer number of writers now engaging in doing it.

Waugh is presumably the most practised modern exemplar, but then his best moments are simply comic; the off-hand brutality seems to get less and less funny in re-reading. Among the golden opinions which Mr Burgess has won, a recurring one is the comparison with Waugh, and it even lured Miss Brooke-Rose into an iambic line: "A Waugh without the underlying wounds." But then if he hasn't the wounds, need he have the casually "comic" violence and pain? The blurb of *The Doctor Is Sick* pointed out that it is "fundamentally more light-hearted than his previous ones" — that is, the story is just that of a man who is waiting for an operation on a brain tumour, who escapes from the hospital and the suffering it inflicts, who sees — or dreams he sees — his wife copulating, and so on. Of course there are straightforward comic things in that book; one of the best (allusive as so many of his best jokes are) comes when the hero stares in at a windowful of nudist magazines:

> There was the one Charlie had brought him: *Brute Beauty*. And there were others he had never seen before: *Valour; Act; Oh!* He rubbed his eyes, which were troubling him with an odd impairment of vision. Were those really *Air, Pride, Plume, Here?*

Anyone who has had enough of "The Windhover" will think that Hopkins has had that coming to him for a long time. But that doesn't alter the fact that it would take stupendous powers to be able to yoke such heterogeneous material together, such pain and such humour. It is the same with *A Clockwork Orange,* an excellent book in so far as it protested against the idea that it is all right to "cure" people of unfortunate tendencies by giving them emetic drugs and showing them films of their undesirable behaviour. (One thinks of the bulletins from the *Observer* which we're still getting about the "cured" homosexual.) But far too much of *A Clockwork Orange* was desperate straddling, and what did its blurb mean by saying that "the book can be read as a straight horror comedy"? Straight? We could do worse than return to the dull neo-classical idea that realistic horror and comedy are different genres. At any rate, *Honey for the Bears* shows how much more Mr Burgess can get said when he isn't also teetering in that rather meaningless and fashionable juggling act.

WILLIAM H. PRITCHARD

The Novels of Anthony Burgess

> Let the strict Life of graver Mortals be
> A long, exact, and serious Comedy,
> In ev'ry Scene some Moral let it teach,
> And, if it can, at once both Please and Preach.
>
> —POPE

Anthony Burgess published his first novel in 1956, his most recent one
in the present year, a fact which becomes of interest only when it is added
that in the intervening period he published fourteen additional novels.
No doubt the figure is already dated for there are no signs of slowing
down; in a recent apologetic valedictory to reviewing theater for *The
Spectator* he confessed ruefully to not having written a novel in six months
or more. One raises an eyebrow at all this plenty, yet only one of the novels
marks itself off as a casual, slight creation, nor does the astonishing rate of
production signal slapdash composition. The five novels selected for consideration here represent a judgment of his best "early" and "later" work;
no doubt any admirer will have his particular favorite to add to the list.
Burgess is a comic writer, a term broad and common enough to cover supposed refinements of it such as satire, grotesque, or farce. None of the
labels substantially promotes understanding of his work, nor does the
knowledge that he, like all British comic novelists, is "the funniest...
since Evelyn Waugh." If comparisons are desired, one would begin with the
guess that the contemporary novelist Burgess most admires is Nabokov;

From *The Massachusetts Review* 3, no. 3 (Summer 1966). © 1966 by The Massachusetts
Review, Inc.

beyond that one goes to Joyce, to Dickens, ultimately to Shakespeare as the literary examples most insistently behind his work. In *Nothing Like the Sun,* his novel about Shakespeare, the hero sees himself as a "word man," and his author is not likely to quarrel with the term as a description of himself. But then, like Nabokov or Joyce or Dickens or Shakespeare, he is more than just a word man: the brilliant exploration of a verbal surface will lead to the discovery of truths about life, of inward revelation. Or will it, does it in fact lead to such truths in the unfolding of Burgess's best work? The question is an interesting one to entertain, though only after we have first been moved and delighted by the books themselves and the continuing presence of their author.

I

Burgess is at his most direct and perhaps most simply appealing in his early novels about life in Malaya just before independence; published last year as a trilogy, *The Long Day Wanes,* the books are given continuity through the presence of Victor Crabbe, an embattled liberal school-master for whom things get progressively worse. Crabbe is one of us: reasonable, guilt-ridden, alternately shabby and decent in his relations with others. In a word, colorless, though he looks colorless only when put next to the characters that surround him, grotesques such as Nabby Adams, an enormous police-official whose life is devoted to the insuring each day of his proximity to about two-dozen bottles of Tiger beer (*Time for a Tiger* is the first volume of the trilogy). Or, emerging from the words themselves, Crabbe's boss Talbot, married to a young and adulterous wife, but truly wedded to his stomach:

> "My dear fellow, you ought to eat. That's the trouble with my wife. Thin as a rake, because she won't bother to order any-thing. She says she's not hungry. I'm always hungry. The climate has different effects on different people. I always have my lunch out. There's a little Chinese place where they give you a really tasty and filling soup, packed with chicken and abalone and vegetables, with plenty of toast and butter, and then I always have a couple of baked crabs."
> "Yes," said Crabbe.
> "With rice and chili sauce. And then a pancake or so, rather soggy, but I don't dislike them that way, with jam and a kind of whipped cream they serve in a tea-cup. Anne, what is there to eat?"

Crabbe's mild "Yes" is a typical Fred Allen response to the antics performed by assorted characters throughout the trilogy. But we are asked to take Crabbe, unlike Fred Allen, seriously as a person. He is presented as a recognizably psychological figure, available for easy identification with on the part of any ordinary reader; his death terminates the trilogy and should evoke some feelings on our part. But the feelings do not appear. We accept Crabbe's fate, whatever it is, without much interest, because we are being so royally entertained elsewhere.

Robert Garis has demonstrated brilliantly how the art of entertainment, as it appears in Dickens's novels, is typically a "loud and distinct" one, apprehended firmly and easily by the reader. In what Garis terms Dickens's "theatrical" art, the reader is happy to watch the artist-showman at his performance, and does not expect to receive complex insights into characters who have to be "taken seriously" as we take Anna Karenina or Dorothea Brooke seriously. The satisfied reader of Dickens delights in the showman's ability energetically to command a large and various number of acts by an inexhaustibly creative language. Burgess's comedy, particularly in his early novels, if not as loud and distinct (or expansive and assured) as Dickens's, is as purely verbal in its workings; for example, all we need or want to know of the glutton Talbot is that he is gluttonous and that his poems are filled with highly nutritious images: we are satisfied to watch the pancakes and whipped-cream roll by. Or to delight with Nabby Adams in his acquiring, without payment, eight large unopened bottles of Tiger beer, and in his anticipation of "The hymeneal gouging-off of the bottle-top, the kiss of the brown bitter yeasty flow, the euphoria far beyond the release of detumescence." The novel-reader's desire to find out what happens next does not assert itself, for the narrator is in no hurry to press on toward exciting revelations. He contemplates instead, with the satisfaction of Nabby Adams viewing the bottles of Tiger, his own agile high-humored creations.

One of the most original and satisfying elements of Burgess's theatricality is a persistent literary allusiveness that teases us to make something out of it and then mocks our efforts. *The Long Day Wanes* invokes Tennyson's "Ulysses," but is Victor Crabbe an "idle king" who eventually drowns in the "deep [that] moans round with many voices"? Only a solemn explicator would be interested in displaying that connection, for the theatrical novelist is less interested in creating symbolic expressions of a complex truth about man than in making play with the words of writers who have expressed such truths. Although the trilogy is filled with allusions to *The Waste Land,* their interest does not lie in suggesting that Victor Crabbe fears death by water (he does), but in the purely amusing way they are woven into the narrative and made to seem at once absurdly confected and perfectly natural: "This music crept by Syed Omar in Police Headquarters, sitting puzzled while others were going out to lunch." As Crabbe's wife reads *The Waste Land* to Nabby Adams and his Malayan sidekick, Nabby remarks

> "He's got that wrong about the pack of cards, Mrs. Crabbe. There isn't no card called The Man With Three Staves. That card what he means is just an ordinary three, like as it may be the three of clubs."

And when they came to the dark thunder-speaking finale of the poem, Alladad Khan nodded gravely.

> *"Datta. Dayadhvam. Damyata.*
> *Shantih. Shantih. Shantih."*

> "He says he understands that bit, Mrs. Crabbe. He says that's what the thunder says."

This "contributes" nothing to the novel except as one more of the witty satisfactions which occur throughout the trilogy. The long day has indeed waned, and the play made with Eliot or Joyce shows us just how late in the game we are, how far from the epic worlds of our modern legendary authors. Far enough it seems so that we can be entertained by a contemporary's familiar use of them.

These isolated examples of entertainment have little to do with the presentation of the hero, Crabbe, who is brought eventually (like all Burgess's heroes) to some sort of reckoning. Typically, the reckoning involves a sexual humiliation; in this novel, Crabbe learns a shocking fact about his first love, then slips into the water while trying to board a launch. We view this event through the impassive gaze of a Malayan doctor who lets him drown, deciding that "Human lives were not his professional concern." There is no other significant comment on the scene. Although it is perfectly well to say that Crabbe is essentially a device for holding together loosely-related characters and episodes, he is also allowed an inner life we must take seriously — his psychological anxieties are given full expression. When it comes to ending the trilogy, the author doesn't seem to know how seriously he wants to take that life, so it is easier to show up the Malayan doctor's sophistry (if it is that), than to assign significance, however minor, to Crabbe's end. It may seem pedantic to accuse Burgess of trying to have it both ways, since *The Long Day Wanes* is a comedy of humours in which, with the exception of Crabbe's story, the narration is external and detached. But the problem is there, and it becomes more complicated when the theatrical novelist does his tricks through a first-person narrator.

This narrator appears as J. W. Denham in what is surely Burgess's most engaging novel, *The Right to an Answer* (1960). A civil servant in the Far East home on holiday in England for much of the book, Denham is over forty, has bad teeth and a cushy job, and can smell the TV-corruption of England in the late fifties. England is a mess because people have too much freedom, and Denham claims to have learned from Hobbes that you can't have both freedom and stability. By the end of the novel he does not pronounce on matters with the arrogant certainty of the opening pages, but it would be wrong to conclude, therefore, that Burgess has written a moral novel with a dramatic change of view. How much, really, can a narrator learn who early in the book talks this way about Sunday dinner at his sister's:

> There was a smell of old dog in the hall, an earthy rebuke at least to the blurry misty pictures of dream-dogs on the walls. The honest black telephone shone coyly from behind flowery curtains — Beryl's homemade booth for long comfy talkie-talkies with women friends, if she had any. I noticed a poker-work poem of slack form and uplifting content: "In a world of froth and bubble two things stand like stone: kindness in another's trouble, courage in your own." Beryl's unimpaired high-school humour was indicated by a framed macaronic paradigm: "Je me larf, tu te grin, il se giggle; nous nous crackons, vouv vous splittez, ils se bustent." Beryl herself could be heard singing in the kitchen at the end of the hall — an emasculated version of "Greensleeves" — and the fumes of heavy greens gushed out under the noise of the masher.

And on and on. Crackling with wordy Nabokovian irritation, the writing individuates Beryl so firmly that there is no temptation to see her as a representative of England's corruption. If this is satire, it is satire which, as Eliot would say, creates the object that it contemplates. Beryl's house is as unforgettably there as the love-nest Lolita's mother designs for Humbert. In neither case are we interested in using the descriptions to censure the ladies in some moral way; by the same token, any claims the narrator makes about his own moral progress will have to compete with his continuous and self-contained verbal brilliance.

At one point in the novel, Denham, playing the inept narrator, apologizes for the lack of action in his tale: "you have had merely J. W. Denham on leave, eating, drinking, unjustifiably censorious, meeting people, especially Mr. Raj, recounting, at the tail of the eye, almost out of earshot, the adultery of small uninteresting people." Mr. Raj is an eager sociologist from Colombo who comes to Denham's home town to investigate the manners and to court an English woman. His most notable capabilities, however, are pugilistic and culinary: in Ted Arden's Shakespearean pub, Mr. Raj disposes of a vocal racist, and Ted muses as follows: " 'Queer bugger that is. It Jack Brownlow, quick as a flash, right in the goolies. . . . I didn't let on when e did it so quick like. E did it real gentleman like.' " Eventually Mr. Raj moves in with Denham and his father, to cook Sunday afternoon curries that are too rich and deep for tears:

> We fell to. My father spooned in curry and panted. He frequently tried to stagger to the kitchen for fresh glasses of cold water, but Mr. Raj said, "No, no. I will get. This is my privilege, Mr. Denhams both." To my father all this was a new world; he ate with Renaissance child's eyes of wonder. "I'd no idea," he gasped. "Never thought." He was like a youth having his first sexual experience.

But all these pleasant events are shattered abruptly as Denham resumes his job in the East and leaves his father in the hands of Mr. Raj, who proceeds to kill him with the kindness of curry. This is one of a series of violent acts, including assault, rape, murder, and the suicide of Mr. Raj, which cause Denham to reexamine his early superiority to "the mess." Although after Mr. Raj's suicide Denham moralizes that these are "just silly vulgar people uncovering the high explosive that lies hidden underneath stability" he is allowed a meditation in the concluding chapter which places him in a different relation to these people. Denham disgustedly contemplates his body in the mirror, then moves to his equally unsatisfactory spirit:

> It was the eyes I didn't like, the unloving mouth, and the holier-than-thou set of the nostrils. . . . The mess was there, the instability, but I wondered now if that sin against stability was really the big sin. What I did realize quite clearly was the little I'd helped, the blundering or not-wishing-to-be-involved plump moneyed man of leave inveighing against sins

he wasn't in the position even to begin to commit. For surely that sneered-at surburban life was more stable than this shadow life of buying and selling in a country where no involvement was possible, the television evening, with the family round, better than the sordid dalliance that soothed me after work?... If poor bloody innocent little Winterbottom had died, and striving Mr. Raj... surely it was something that they invoked the word Love? Even the word was better than this emptiness, this standing on the periphery and sneering.

This seems to offer us a secure vantage-point from which to review the events with understanding. But are we convinced by it? What indeed would it mean to be "convinced" by it? Doesn't the analysis unjustly simplify Denham's earlier behavior, since the behavior has been presented to us through a style which delights? How can we accept "sneering" or "standing on the periphery" as adequate labels for the description of Beryl's house quoted earlier? Or, from the same chapter, is the following menu a sneer at the English Sunday meal?

The meal was pretentious—a kind of beetroot soup with greasy *croûtons*; pork underdone with loud vulgar cabbage, potato croquettes, tinned peas in tiny jam-tart cases, watery gooseberry sauce; trifle made with a resinous wine, so jammy that all my teeth lit up at once—a ghastly discord on two organ manuals.

One quickly grows fond of those encased peas, that loud cabbage; the food, through these words, becomes not just awful but fascinatingly awful. Here, as in general, the imaginative vitality of Denham-Burgess's prose elbows aside the moralist who later repents of his hypercritical satiric self.

Denham's relationship to "the mess, the instability" represents a novelistic questioning of the satirist's relationship to life, to the materials of fiction. *The Right to an Answer* is unique in Burgess's work for the way it shows an aggressively comic and satiric intelligence taking us in through a casual first-person style of reporting. At the same time, or perhaps as a result of such aggressive dealing, the "I" repents of it, apologizes to us for putting himself outside the reek of the human. I am really no better than they are, probably not as good, he winningly admits. But if the apology is an engaging gesture of humility, it has things both ways only through a noticeable straining in the very prose of the book. When the narrator refers harshly, in the above passage, to "the sordid dalliance that soothed me after work," just how seriously can we take something which is referred to by a demonstrably witty intelligence as "sordid dalliance"? And does Burgess himself know how seriously he wants to take it? The attempt by a marvelous entertainer to discover a truth about life, to engage in moral reappraisal of himself, results in an uncomfortable sleight-of-hand effect that isn't quite quick enough to escape our notice. And the question remains: how much can the dark comedian afford to enlighten, with sincere reflection, the chaotic scene he has so wittily imagined?

II

This question, asked by the critic, is of course one the artist is under no obligation to answer. Burgess goes on to publish three novels (*Devil of a State, The Worm and the Ring, The Doctor Is Sick*) which in their individually interesting ways avoid the issue and which, for all their excellent goings-on, are not as solidly entertaining as *The Long Day Wanes*, or as humanly ambitious as *The Right to an Answer*. It is the three novels that appear in 1962–63 which present a truly experimental attempt to unite brilliance of entertainment with a seriousness toward human beings — more accurately, toward humanity. *A Clockwork Orange, The Wanting Seed*, and *Honey for the Bears* are (at least the first and last) Burgess's most popular books and they ask to be considered together. All of them concern the individual and the modern state; all of them are felt to have a connection with the quality of life in the 1960s, but they approach life obliquely by creating fantasies or fables which appeal to us in odd and disturbing ways. As always with Burgess's work, and now to a splendidly bizarre degree, the creativity is a matter of style, of words combined in strange new shapes. Through the admiration these shapes raise, rather than through communication of specifiable political, philosophical or religious ideas about man or the state, is to be found the distinction of these novels; for this reason it is of limited use to invoke names like Huxley or Orwell as other novelists of imagined futurist societies.

A Clockwork Orange, most patently experimental of the novels, is written in a language created by combining Russian words with teenage argot into a hip croon that sounds both ecstatic and vaguely obscene. The hero, Alex, a teen-age thug, takes his breakfast and morning paper this way:

> And there was a bolshy big article on Modern Youth (meaning
> me, so I gave the old bow, grinning like bezoomny) by some

very clever bald chelloveck. I read this with care, my brothers, slurping away at the old chai, cup after tass after chasha, crunching my lomticks of black toast dipped in jammiwam and eggiweg. This learned veck said the usual veshches, about no parental discipline, as he called it, and the shortage of real horrorshow teachers who would lambast bloody beggary out of their innocent poops and make them go boohoohoo for mercy. All this was gloopy and made me smeck, but it was nice to go on knowing one was making the news all the time, O my brothers.

Although the American paperback edition provides a glossary, one doesn't need it to get along very well after the first few pages. In fact such translation is a mistake for it short-circuits the unmistakable rhythms of speech by which the sentences almost insensibly assume meaning. Moreover, though the book is filled with the most awful violence — what in our glossary or newspaper would be called murder, assault, rape, perversion — it comes to us through an idiom that, while it does not deny the connection between what happens in the second chapter and what the newspaper calls a "brutal rape," nevertheless makes what happens an object of aesthetic interest in a way no rape can or should be. Life — a dreadful life to be sure — is insistently and joyously deflected into the rhythms of a personal style within which one eats lomticks, not pieces, of toast.

The novel is short and sharply plotted: Alex is betrayed by his fellow "droogs," imprisoned for murder, then by a lobotomizing technique is cured of his urges to violence; whereas music, Beethoven in particular, had inspired him to heights of blood-lusts, he now just feels sick. Caught between the rival parties for state power he tries suicide, but lives to recover his original identity, as listening to the scherzo of the Beethoven Ninth he sees himself "carving the whole litso of the creeching world with my cut-throat britva." The book concludes on this happy note, for oddly enough it *is* a happy note; we share the hero's sense of high relief and possibility, quite a trick for the novelist to have brought off. And without questioning it we have acceded to the book's "message," as radical and intransigent as the style through which it is expressed:

More, badness is of the self, the one, the you or me on our oddy knockies, and that self is made by old Bog or God and is his great pride and radosty. But the not-self cannot have the bad, meaning they of the government and the judges and the schools cannot allow the bad because they cannot allow the self. And is not our modern history, my brothers, the story of brave malenky selves fighting these big machines. I am serious with you, brothers, over this. But what I do I do because I like to do.

Doing what you do because you like to do it is what the Burgess hero — Crabbe, Denham, others — has done and had been punished for doing by his creator. But the hero of *A Clockwork Orange* is rewarded and endorsed in a way more recognizably human characters in a more "realistic" atmosphere could not possible be. In the world of creative fantasy we can admire hero and event as they are shaped by language; our response is akin to the old-fashioned "admiration" proper to the heroic poem. By the same token the defense of self, no matter how twisted it may be, and the condemnation of the state, no matter now benevolent it pretends to be, is absolute. Such a simple and radical meaning is not morally complex, but it must be taken as a serious aspect of fantasy. Within its odd but carefully observed limits the book is entirely consistent, successful and even pleasing, Burgess's most eye- and ear-catching performance.

Published a few months later, *The Wanting Seed* pleased critics a good deal less, the general feeling being that Burgess had overreached himself and produced a hodge-podge book. It is true that nothing is alien to its virtuoso atmosphere: elemental poetry, broad jokes, science fiction and political philosophy consort together, couched throughout in a highly pedantic and jawbreaking vocabulary ("corniculate," "vexillae," "fritinancy," "parachronic"). But in this most Joycean of Burgess's novels, that virtuoso atmosphere is precisely what appeals. The novel takes the population explosion as fictional opportunity and imagines a society presided over by a Ministry of Infertility which encourages homosexuality ("It's Sapiens to be Homo" is their motto) and forbids any woman to bear more than one child. As in *A Clockwork Orange* the lawless individual is at odds with a "benevolent" state; the heroine, Beatrice-Joanna, married to Tristram Foxe, a history teacher, is having an affair with Tristram's brother, a government official. Beatrice-Joanna's rebellion consists in her refusal to accept the death of her son and her rejection of the doctor's sensible advice: "Think of this in national terms, in global terms. One mouth less to feed. One more half-kilo of phosphorus pentoxide to nourish the earth. In a sense, you know, Mrs. Foxe, you'll be getting your son back again." Emerging from the clinic, she walks down the great London street (once Brighton but now a part of Greater London) to the sea and perceives it with a special poetry granted her:

> If only, she felt crazily, poor Roger's body could have been thrown into these tigrine waters, swept out to be gnawed by

fish, rather than changed coldly to chemicals and silently fed to the earth. She had a mad intuitive notion that the earth was dying, that the sea would soon be the final repository of life. "Vast sea gifted with delirium, panther skin and mantle pierced with thousands of idols of the sun—" She had read that somewhere, a translation from one of the auxiliary languages of Europe. The sea drunk with its own blue flesh, a hydra, biting its tail.

Then looking up at the Government Building she sees the figure of a bearded man: "A cynosure to ships, man of the sea, Pelagius. But Beatrice-Joanna could remember a time when he had been Augustine. And, so it was said, he had been at other times the King, the Prime Minister, a popular bearded guitarist, Eliot (a long-dead singer of infertility), the Minister of Pisciculture, captain of the Hertfordshire Men's Sacred Game eleven, and most often and satisfactorily—the great unknown, the magical Anonymous." A hodge-podge of style perhaps, but no more so than *Ulysses:* at one moment the scientific knowingness of a Buck Mulligan, then the moody broodings of Stephen Dedalus, followed by an inventive Bloomlike list. What holds the various styles together is a linguistic virtuoso who moves his characters up and down the map of England: to complain as one reviewer did that the hero and heroine were mechanical contrivances is not to the point, since more "character," more recognizably human dimension, would destroy the fable.

For proof of this, consider the block of chapters describing Tristram's attempt to join his wife in the North of England (he has just escaped from jail and she, pregnant, has fled to her brother-in-law, an old-fashioned Roman Catholic, to have what turns out to be twins). As the state moves from a Pelagian phase to an Augustinian one, a great famine impels man toward cannibalism, fertility rites, the genesis of drama, and from homo- to heterosexual love. Tristram observes these effects as he moves from Brighton to Wigan, but we have heard reports of them already, courtesy of Anthony Burgess the announcer:

> In Stoke-on-Trent the carcass of a woman (later identified as Maria Bennett, spinster, aged twenty-eight) grinned up suddenly—several good clean cuttings off her—from under a bank of snow. In Gillingham, Kent, Greater London, a shady back-street eating-shop opened, grilling nightly, and members of both police forces seemed to patronize it. In certain unregenerate places on the Suffolk coast there were rumours of big

> crackling Christmas dinners. . . . The New Year commenced
> with stories of timid anthropophagy. . . . Then the metro-
> polis flashed its own sudden canines: a man called Amis suf-
> fered savage amputation of an arm off Kingsway; S. R. Coke,
> journalist, was boiled in an old copper near Shepherd's Bush;
> Miss Joan Waine, a teacher, was fried in segments.

Some might consider this (especially the reference to imagined fates of
Angries) a debilitating cleverness, fatal to Burgess's art; to me it seems admirably indigenous to his ruthlessly literary sensibility. But in any case, it
must be agreed that an attempt to give a hero traveling through such a
scene much "dimension" would result in an awkward and uncertain
book. *The Wanting Seed* is neither: its inventiveness is large enough that
we are content to follow the fortunes of heroine and hero without desir-
ing some further "inward" reach of understanding. What is to be understood—taken in—is put before us in the theatrical manner spoken of
earlier. Even the closing paragraphs of the book, coming as they do after
the longest of journeys and bringing together the Tristram Foxes and
their twins, united on the promenade at Brighton, even these paragraphs
are less a moving tribute to a particular man or woman than they are a
general and now mythicized embodiment of love, of possibility:

> She clung to him, the huge air, the life-giving sea, man's
> future history in the depths, the present towered town, the
> bearded man at the pinnacle, all shut out from the warmth of
> his presence, the closeness of his embrace. He became sea,
> sun, tower. The twins gurgled. There were still no words.

And as if to formalize and make shimmery this closing atmosphere, the
narrator dons prophetic robes and plays a late Shakespearean sage or Joycean lyricist, in language stolen from Valéry:

> The wind rises . . . we must try to live. The immense air
> opens and closes my book. The wave, pulverized, dares to
> gush and spatter from the rocks. Fly away, dazzled, blinded
> pages. Break, waves. Break with joyful waters.

This looks more vulnerable in quotation than it feels in the act of finishing
the novel, although one understands how such writing might give rise to
distrust or scepticism about its narrative poise. Burgess knows the extrava-
gant overreaching that attaches to grand incantations, and as a rule his
fictions do not make them. But *The Wanting Seed*, like *A Clockwork*

Orange, has its affinities with the herioc poem: "faring forward" is saluted by the Bard when he ends his tale with an imitative gesture meant just as seriously as the cannibalistic jokes inspected earlier. In creative fantasy or fable, no suggestion that its figures are merely human is in order: Alex prepares to resume his career as a hoodlum; Beatrice-Joanna and Tristram prepare for—what? The fact is we are not interested in these "characters," only the action in which they have figured. A reader of *The Wanting Seed* must vouch to the extent that, like it or not, it is very much a linguistic action.

By contrast, *Honey for the Bears* would seem to be a return to the real world—the Soviet Union in 1963—where Paul Hussey, an English antique dealer, and his American wife Belinda are engaged in smuggling in and selling twenty-dozen drilon dresses, the loot for which will be turned over to the widow of a dead friend. A mysterious rash sends Belinda to the hospital where she falls under the influence of a female Dr. Lazurkina who analyzes Paul as a homosexual ("gomosexual" without the "h" in Russian) and spirits Belinda off to the Crimea for what promises to be a long talk. Paul makes his own liaison with a bearded young Russian strugling to be hip and properly disenchanted about the modern state: " 'Russia or America,' said Alexei Prutkov, 'what's the difference? It's all the State. There's only one State. What we have to do is get together in these little groups and start to live.' " But after an unsuccessful attempt by Paul to seduce Alexei's mistress, and a drunken party where Paul suggests the guests strip "stark ballock naked," he is thrown out of Alexei's group with the accusation "What you like, dig, is your own sex, and that's what's so filthy and disgusting." Other humiliations and confusions follow (teeth knocked out, thrown into prison) until Paul leaves Russia, this time smuggling out (as his wife) the son of a Russian composer in disgrace named Opiskin, whose works Paul's dead friend Robert had loved.

It makes little difference whether we call this "plot" (inadequately summarized here) brilliant or absurd, so long as the detailing of it removes all suspicion that Burgess has abandoned us to Real Life in the Soviet Union today. *Honey for the Bears* is just as fantastic or fabulous as its two predecessors; characters (possibly excepting the hero) are viewed externally as ever, and their dimensions (and our sympathies) are thus severely limited. Stylistically the book moves at whirlwind pace with events and thoughts rapidly telescoped through Paul Hussey's mind; for example, on the first page we have this response to an unknown aged master in a wheelchair:

The face was trenched and riven, as by a killing life of

> metaphysical debauchery. That was it, decided Paul: a head
> that philosophy had unsexed, some final Shavian achieve-
> ment. He had seen a head like it on television newsreels; an
> old proud eagle squatting in Whitehall among students, Ban-
> ning the Bomb. But these oyster-coloured eyes surveyed with
> disdain the scruffy redbrick layabouts who nearly filled the
> Cultural Saloon, the nose twitched at them.

Paul's own "unsexing" is to come, when by the end of the book he admits
that he no longer knows what he is, sexually. And so the novel invites us,
as did the earlier *Right to an Answer,* to relate the satiric intelligence ac-
corded Paul in the passage above, to something he learns in Russia; more
generally, to feel a unifying of the style of entertainment with the content
of truth.

In the best single piece of writing about Burgess ("The Epicene,"
New Statesman, April 5, 1963) Christopher Ricks argues that this can be
done, insofar as the book makes an analogy between sexual and political
behavior. Politically the book presents America and Russia as equally
monolithic and insufficient states, and opts instead for what Ricks calls a
"Third Force." So, by analogy, homo- and heterosexuality need not be
exclusive choices; without singing hymns to bisexuality it can at least be
entertained and admitted to be perhaps more fun, more attractive to the
individual who would be free. Ricks points out correctly that this is a subversive message, but that it is transmitted in an "inventive and gay" manner that takes the fear out of it. And he goes on to claim that the book is
more humane and "says more" than Burgess's earlier minglings of black
violence with comic lightness. It would be pleasant to take *Honey for the
Bears* as evidence of this kind of novelistic breakthrough, especially since
at the moment it is the most recent full-fledged novel Burgess has given
us. But it is much more problematic than Ricks suggests whether the
"message" about sex and about politics is convincingly worked into the
texture of the novel. There are difficulties in knowing just how to take
Paul's sexual humiliations with his wife and Alexei's mistress—they are
indeed fiascos, but do not recommend themselves to us as, in book-jacket
language, "outrageously funny" or "wildly comic." They are no more
comic than Paul's difficulty in keeping his false teeth in place. On the
other hand the narrator makes no attempt to extend Paul sympathetic
understanding. We are free, if we choose, to connect heterosexual failure
with Paul's memories of "poor, dead Robert," though these memories are
sentimental moonings we assume the narrator doesn't fully share. But

even this is an assumption. Burgess treats Paul any way the spirit moves him: now harshly, now pathetically, now as a witty, perceptive satirical eye — all depending on the exigencies of a moment. When we try to say what these moments add up to the trouble begins. What they claim to add up to is concentrated in two passages late in the novel: in the first of these, Paul relates a dream to his cell-mates about how there was a little man who lived between two greatly opposing tsardoms. They bully the little man by giving him a wife who accuses him of not being a real man, an adequate protector. Like Belinda, the wife walks out. The second passage makes the Paul-as-England identification explicit: "I'm going back to an antique-shop, but somebody's got to conserve the good of the past, before your Americanism and America's Russianism make plastic of the world. . . . You'll learn about freedom from us yet." Even as he says it he feels a "doubt," as does surely the reader. For England (Rick's polit-ical "Third Force"?) is simply not *there* in the novel, any more than is Paul Hussey's inner life which, we are told, has undergone some sort of change. Once more, the imagination of comic disorder proves stronger than the fable's attempt to make thoughtful sense out of it.

This is not cause for alarm, nor a gloomy note on which to conclude. When Ricks says, in the essay mentioned above, that Burgess has yet to write a really "first-rate comic novel" we may feel the standards are high indeed after reading through a group of novels distinguished by their abundant qualities of imaginative energy, creative invention, compli-cated wit, and verbal delight. Since *Honey for the Bears* Anthony Burgess has given us a number of books somewhat off-the-center of his literary vi-sion: juvenilia, a fascinating novelistic sport about Shakespeare, books on language and on Joyce. In a recent *Times Literary Supplement* article titled "The Manicheans" he mused aloud on why the novel has not made more use of religious experience, and he specified further:

> I do not mean the tribulations of priests among the poor, or
> deanery gossip, or pre-ordination doubts; I mean rather the
> imaginative analysis of themes like sainthood, sin, the escha-
> tological sanctions of behaviour, even that dangerous beatific
> vision.

One of the best ways to analyze sin is to become a comic novelist; there is every reason to suspect that the remaining themes will occupy Burgess in the novels to come. At any rate we can be grateful for the books we have. After Nabokov there is no other, but that is because, in part, Nabokov sees the world through imaginatively obsessed narrator-madmen who

impose their strange shapes on reality. Burgess, despite the variety of narra-
tors and situations in his fiction, speaks to us as one of us: a fallen man with
the usual amount of ambition, irritation, guilt, decency and common
sense. Given such ordinary qualities or modest sins, how can things go as
wrong as they do for the heroes of these painful books? That they go not
just wrong, but marvelously wrong, is the result of the one quality Burgess
does not share with the rest of us or with his heroes — the art of the novelist.

CHARLES G. HOFFMANN AND A. C. HOFFMANN

Mr. Kell and Mr. Burgess: Inside and Outside Mr. Enderby

The recent publication of *Enderby Outside* (1968) by Anthony Burgess completes the portrait of Enderby begun in *Inside Mr. Enderby* (1963) but originally published under the pseudonym of Joseph Kell. The dust-jacket blurb of the English edition of *Enderby Outside,* repeated in the one-volume American edition of the two Enderby novels, maintains the fiction that Mr. Kell and Mr. Burgess are two separate authors and that Kell, having died, bequeathed to Burgess "Not merely his copyrights and royalties but also his identity. His dying wish was that Mr. Burgess should conclude the story about Enderby, the poet, already half-told in *Inside Mr. Enderby.*" Although Joseph Kell "died in 1966 when the Penguin edition of *Inside Mr. Enderby* was published under the name of Anthony Burgess, the fiction about the identities of Mr. Kell and Mr. Burgess is more than a private joke between publisher and author who know that both names are pseudonyms for John Anthony Burgess Wilson, a retired Colonial Service education officer. It is a recognition of the fact that Wilson has established his reputation and come into his own as a novelist under the name of Burgess, a literary identity he never achieved as Joseph Kell.

The significance of the "pseudo-pseudonym" of Joseph Kell lies not in its frankly admitted original intention of hiding over-production (Anthony Burgess, for that is now his public identity, has published seventeen novels since 1956, all but three of them in the past eight years). It lies in

From *The Shaken Realist: Essays in Modern Literature in Honor of Frederick J. Hoffmann,* edited by Melvin J. Friedman and John B. Vickery. ©1970 by Louisiana State University Press.

the fact that the two strands of Burgess's art, the comic and the tragic, become one vision in the Enderby novels, a black comedy of the contemporary scene. Long before the publication of *Inside Mr. Enderby*, Burgess had created a purely comic novel about life in the British army stationed on Gibraltar at the end of the Second World War, *A Vision of Battlements*, which although not published until 1965 was written in 1949. And he had already explored the dark side of life in the Malayan trilogy — *Time for a Tiger* (1956), *The Enemy in the Blanket* (1958), *Beds in the East* (1959) — and probed the illnesses of contemporary English civilization in *The Right to an Answer* (1960) and *The Doctor Is Sick* (1960). From the beginning Burgess has possessed as sharp an eye for the ridiculous and ludicrous in human behavior as he has sensitive an ear for the speech rhythms of his characters whether Malayan or English, Cockney or public school. This comic sense of the absurd in human actions tends to overshadow the essentially tragic vision he intended to portray in the life and death of the protagonist of the Malayan trilogy, Victor Crabbe. For example, the farcical situations involving Victor Crabbe's infidelities belie the depth of his guilt feelings toward his second wife, Fenella, compounded by his guilt at having killed his first wife in an automobile accident. In *A Clockwork Orange* (1962) and *The Wanting Seed* (1962) the tragic vision dominates, and although there is comic relief in clever puns and witty slogans, the comedy intensifies the horror of unbridled juvenile violence and unchecked governmental authoritarianism. It was in *One Hand Clapping* (1961), the only other novel beside *Inside Mr. Enderby* published under the name of Joseph Kell, that Burgess attempted to fuse the two sides of his creative vision, and failed.

Taking its title from a play the protagonists, Howard and Janet Shirley, attend — "a play dealing with the decay and decadence in the world about us" — *One Hand Clapping* satirizes the decadent world of supermarkets, television quiz shows, secondary modern schools, council houses, washing machines, vacuum cleaners, all the visible goods that add quantity but not quality to contemporary English life, circa 1960. The phrase "one hand clapping" originates in Zen Buddhism and is, Howard explains, "a way of getting in touch with Reality, you see, proceeding by way of the absurd. . . . It's supposed to be a way of getting to God."

Contemporary English life as portrayed in the novel is absurd and materialistic, having substituted Money for God, symbolized by the television quiz show on which Howard wins a large amount of money because he has a photographic memory. With his winnings Howard sets out to prove that Money is a false God, not in the tradition of the biblical prophets but on its own ground, proving that in a mass-produced economy materialism cannot give value or quality for its money. Howard comes to the conclusion that death, self-willed and self-inflicted, is the only way to Reality in the modern world. He decides he will commit suicide after first killing his wife, but Janet kills him because she wants to "live," totally accepting the values of the society Howard has rejected.

The novel's failure as a satire is largely that of Burgess's choice of narrator. Janet Shirley is a pleasant but dull British housewife who measures her days and accomplishments throughout most of the novel in terms of material possessions, stacking them up like the tins of baked beans in the Hastings Road supermarket where she works. Her uncomprehending naïveté as she recounts the past is equaled by her vapid conclusions when Howard wins the big quiz prize and they can buy anything they desire: the food they eat in fashionable restaurants cannot compare with the tinned delights served by her at home in the Shortshawe Council Estate, and the fast-paced life in the big cities of the world is no more exciting to her than a day spent in the supermarket joking with her fellow workers. Such a narrator cannot be selective, must compulsively give endless and seemingly inconsequential information. Lacking sensitivity and articulateness, Janet Shirley's narration clearly reveals the limitations of the Secondary Modern school system where the teachers assume that the students will not be interested in English and history and therefore entertain them rather than teach them; but although the satiric point is clear, it is made at the sacrifice of complexity and subtlety of insight. Her mind is a *tabula rasa* — she does not discriminate between the minutiae and the important fact imbedded within them — yet she must be the narrator, not Howard who attempts to understand and develop beyond the limitations of his environment but who can only solve his dilemma by the desperate remedy of death. Burgess succeeded in creating a viable plot whose ramifications explore the absurdity of contemporary life, but hampered himself with an implausible narrator whose personality changes three-fourths of the way through the novel from a conventional housewife to a *femme fatale* who is unfaithful to her husband, kills him in self-defense, runs away with her lover (the poet Redvars Glass), who then assumes Howard's name and identity. Together Janet and Redvars accompany Howard's body to France, keeping it in a wardrobe and deciding ultimately to dispose of this encumbrance by using it as a scarecrow! However, the bizarre horror of this act and Janet's thinking at the end that she may have to dispose of Redvars in a similar fashion does suggest one thematic direction

Burgess develops, the anti-utopian world of violence and inhumanity in *A Clockwork Orange* and *The Wanting Seed,* but in *One Hand Clapping* the reader is unprepared for Janet Shirley's shift in character.

If the failure of *One Hand Clapping* as a satiric portrait of modern society is inherent in the mindlessness of its narrator, its failure to achieve a fusion of the comic and the tragic is implicit in the single-minded despair of its hero. There is no tragic conflict between the absurdity of the human condition Howard Shirley rejects and his will to die. A slave to his photographic memory, he lacks an identity by which the inner reality of his self can be tested against the forces of the outside world. Nor can he reach reality by way of the absurd because he lacks the comic vision to encompass the absurd. It is certain he will die — the only suspense is whether he will take his wife Janet with him — but his death is not at the hands of fate, and Janet who strikes the blow that kills him is no agent of fate. His death is the physical end of a death of the mind that antedates the narrative time of the novel, for he is, except for the quirk of his memory, as much a product of the civilization he has rejected as Janet who accepts it.

Burgess's failure to provide Howard Shirley with an identity by which the comic and the tragic could be combined led him to tackle the problem of identity directly in the Enderby novels. The dust-jacket anecdote about the identities of Mr. Kell and Mr. Burgess reveals, however, coyly, the major theme of the Enderby novels, the quest for identity. In *A Clockwork Orange* the problem of identity for the narrator-protagonist, Alex, becomes the focus of the novel's climax. In the Enderby novels the search for self-identity is central to the entire work, and a multiplicity of identities is the means by which Burgess successfully unites the two sides of his art by creating an interaction between the comic and the tragic vision of life.

Whereas the satire on contemporary life is diffuse throughout and dissipated at the end of *One Hand Clapping,* it is sharp and consistent, although more narrowly focused, in *Inside Mr. Enderby.* The satiric tone of *Inside Mr. Enderby* is set from the beginning in the outer frame which encloses both of the Enderby novels and links them together as a whole. The frame is narrated by a sycophantic teacher-guide whose attempts to pontificate upon the higher meanings of poetry and poets are as far removed from the inner reality of Enderby as his attention to the external details of Enderby's life and surroundings. But the frame narrator's observation that little is known about Enderby because "he was essentially a man who lived inside himself" (speaking in the past tense as a biographer) establishes the theme inherent in the title. Inside, Enderby is the isolated poet completely engrossed by the irrational waxing and waning of his talent that seem to follow the biological rhythms of his viscera. He is the antithesis of the romantic poet inspired by a lofty muse; the process of creation is described in cloacal detail as Enderby, the mid-twentieth-century English poet, sits on a cold toilet seat, an electric fire at his feet, his poems, written on toilet tissue, filling the bathtub. Too much, however, can be made of the scatalogical and visceral details of Enderby's creativity, for Burgess's purpose is not to shock the reader (if indeed the modern reader is shockable) or to deprecate the creative process, but to suggest in the Joycean sense that in the womb the word was made flesh. The privacy of the privy is the only "womb" left for the poet in the modern world with its demand for social identity and social usefulness, the creed represented by the psychiatrists, Drs. Greenslade and Wapenshaw, and given the governmental seal of approval by the National Health Service.

The inward-looking Enderby is no Redvars Glass, although both are poets, for we see Redvars only from the outside as the extrovert, virile, bohemian who betrays Howard Shirley twice, first by cuckolding him and then by violating his role as guest in the Shirley home, turning it over to his indigent friends while the Shirleys are away on their hopeless quest for "all the happiness that money can buy." Nor is Enderby Howard Shirley although he too attempts to commit suicide; Enderby affirms life, if only that of the mind, whereas Shirley, pursued by a self-destructive death-wish, denies life. Enderby inside is happy in the self-imposed limitations of his craft, but Enderby outside is an incomplete man, a Huxleyan character, sexually impotent, socially incompetent, emotionally immature. The dichotomy between the inner reality of his poetic imagination and the outer reality of his social role is too severe, particularly after he leaves the security of his womb and marries the vestal virgin of modern womanhood, Vesta Bainbridge; and Enderby breaks down. However, there is more similarity between Enderby and Howard Shirley than there is between Redvars and Enderby. Both Shirley and Enderby are driven to their fates by the inner necessity of a peculiarity in their mental processes over which they have no control, the one by his photographic memory and the other by his poetic imagination. The "muse" or inner necessity of creativity in Enderby is embodied in a will that is as primitive and natural as his biological functions and is related to them: "The act of creation. Sex. That was the trouble with art. Urgent sexual desire aroused with the excitement of a new image or rhythm." It is because of his arrested development as a social and sexual man that Enderby's creative energies are so rawly and biologically directed in nature. As long as he remains inside the protective womb of his identity as poet, he is, "taking all things into consideration, by and large, not to put too fine a point on it, reasonably well self-sufficient." But the poet's search for Beauty, as man's search for Love, if it is to reach beyond narcissism, is embodied in Woman (even 'Arry the cook recognizes this when he gets Enderby to write love poetry to Thelma the barmaid). Creativity is thus related to the yin-yang motion of the universe, the mysterious forces of life embodied in women. Enderby's search for Beauty is an alternation between the yin and yang of the dark and light forces in his life. His physically repulsive stepmother is the cause of his sexual impotency, yet she is the Muse who provides him with the financial means to cultivate his poetry. But Enderby is unable to accept his Muse as an ugly stepmother who although dead and buried reappears Circe-like in his life in different guises (the drunken woman in the saloon-bar of the Neptune; his landlady, Mrs. Meldrum; Thelma the barmaid; Vesta Bainbridge and finally, Miranda Boland) as he journeys forth on his odyssey in the outside world, returning "home" to the womb-like security of the lavatory. Ironically, it is his mother's maiden name, Hogg, which he assumes for his new identity as the scientifically reconstructed man, the non-poet but socially well-adjusted man. Thus Circe who can turn men into swine as well as into lovers literally turns Enderby into a Hogg, at least that part of him which seeks a normal life in modern society by marrying Vesta under the illusion he was creating a new life, a new beginning for himself.

In a scene that anticipates the Orwellian horror of Alex's reclamation in *A Clockwork Orange,* Enderby is cured of his anti-social identity as a poet and rehabilitated into a socially useful person of service to humanity as a bartender. It is at this point that *Inside Mr. Enderby* ends and *Enderby Outside* begins. Burgess's intention of making the two novels sequential is obvious not only in the titles chosen and in the repetition of the external narrative frame but also in the thematic development of Enderby's two identities. The change from poet to barman is an incomplete metamorphosis; inside the shell of his new identity as Hogg, Enderby the poet, the word-man, exists in Kafkaesque reality, yearning for recognition and love. As Enderby moves from the inner but safer world of poetry to the outer but frightening world of women's magazines, movie scenarios, hip writers, and pop singers, he loses his original identity; for the poet, Burgess implies, is primarily an anti-social, self-sustaining creature who must remain imprisoned in the cave of his own self if he is to remain free to develop his talents. In *Inside Mr. Enderby*, Enderby's attempts to escape the confines of the prison of his art end in disaster — the comic episode of the poet's luncheon in London, the carnival chaos of Rome, the unconsummated marriage to Vesta Bainbridge. But in *Enderby Outside,* Hogg is no more capable of coping with the irrationalities and injustices of life than Enderby was. Accused of murdering Yod Crewsy the modern god (Yahweh) of popular art, Hogg escapes to Tangiers, a fugitive from the wrath of Vesta Bainbridge and the devotees of Yod's Crewsy Fixers whose supposedly martyred leader is resurrected to life as part of a publicity stunt.

Enderby-Hogg can only regain his identity as a poet by assuming a third identity, that of his Nemesis, Rawcliffe, the poet who had borrowed Enderby's poems if not his identity. Enderby's fate is to become a minor poet, for poetry is a minor art in a world that deifies the pop singer Yod Crewsy; that is why Rawcliffe's identity suits Enderby so well, for Rawcliffe has achieved a reputation as a minor poet, mainly on the borrowings from Enderby. In a world where Yod Crewsy is the Son of God the Father, the poet must identify with an earlier mythology; Rawcliffe is Icarus whose dead body is consigned to the sea from an airplane by Enderby, and Enderby, the old artificer Daedalus, Rawcliffe's passport in his pocket, becomes Icarus. Reversing the Joycean motif that the son must displace the father, Burgess suggests that the Creator must become the Son (Logos), the word-man, defying society, rebellious, disobedient, aloof, but yet compassionate and undemanding. Rawcliffe's suffering and death had taught Enderby pity, and he no longer desires revenge against Vesta Bainbridge. He had yet to learn love.

Before Enderby can return to the womb where the word was made flesh, he must trick Circe into giving back his identity as a poet. Circe reappears in *Enderby Outside* in the guise of Miranda Boland, the modern moon goddess, who may not know Greek mythology, failing to recognize the name of Selene, but who knows the science of the moon, being a lecturer in selenography. Enderby is in "disguise" as Enderby, having fled England after the apparent death of Yod Crewsy, dropping the name Hogg and using his Enderby passport to escape. But he is still Hogg the non-poet, poetically impotent, even though he claims to be Enderby the poet. It is at the height of his love-making with Miranda that he regains his poetic gift; "an ejaculation of words" comes. Frustrated and bitter, Miranda penetrates his disguise and recognizes him as Hogg, but it is too late for her; he is in reality Enderby, again poetically potent but still sexually impotent. It is the love of beauty not the love of body that he pursues.

At the end Enderby meets his Muse in the form of a beautiful golden girl, nameless but seductive. Although she offers her body to him, Enderby cannot accept; his sexual impotency is now a recognition that as a poet he must always be seduced by beauty but can never possess beauty for himself. He has learned love, but his love must be a pursuit of ideal beauty not the possession of it. She will inspire him, help him develop a critical judgment for himself, but the beauty he creates will be for others not for himself, just as all his life he has been surrounded by the detritus of other lives, whether it be his stepmother, his landlady, Vesta Bainbridge or Rawcliffe.

Burgess does not disagree [in *The Novel Now*] with those critics who have found three persistent themes in his novels: "the need to laugh in the face of a desperate future; questions of loyalty; the relationships between countries and between races." In fact, most of his novels deal with all three either directly or indirectly, depending upon the emphasis. In the Malayan trilogy the tragi-comic theme of personal loyalty is tightly bound to the theme of relationship between races in the colonies, as is true of *The Right to an Answer,* in which the lives of the English businessman J. W. Denham and the Ceylonese amateur sociologist Mr. Raj become intertwined. Burgess's most successful novels, however, subordinate these themes to a satiric view of man's folly and the absurd society which exploits the blatant and the bad, places a premium upon notoriety and the creation of public idols. Thus, the violent world of the street gang in *A Clockwork Orange* is rendered through a created language which captures the desperate alienation and hopelessness of youth in a materialistic and disintegrating social order. In *The Wanting Seed* Burgess creates an anti-utopian society in which the problem of overpopulation is solved with scientific detachment through the scholastic logic of a bureaucracy. The Enderby novels are a further exploration of these themes as Enderby finds himself betrayed on all sides, must exile himself from the womb that is England and make his way in the irrational world of Tangiers, and "laugh in the face of a desperate future." The comic mask that Burgess wears — the Joycean puns, the absurd situations in which his characters find themselves, the ridiculous antics of his characters — is a desperate laughter in the face of the tragic condition of man — the plight of the artist in the modern world, the violence that underlies the veneer of civilized behavior, the Kafkaesque alienation of the sensitive individual, the Orwellian nightmare of governmental controls, the basic conflict of good and evil. But dark laughter, Burgess's recognition of the absurd in life, becomes Enderby's saving grace, the means by which he achieves identity as a poet, using the absurdities of the world outside as the raw material for poetry. Enderby's odyssey is completed, and he can go "home" having returned Lazarus-like from a living death and renewed his gift as a poet.

ROBERT K. MORRIS

The Bitter Fruits of Freedom

At first blush, *A Clockwork Orange* and *The Wanting Seed* may appear —one because of stylistic shockers, the other for its Gothicism and *grand guignol*—more like bizarre and fantastic companions to the Burgess canon than parts of it. Like the majority of sci-fi trading on metarealities, the novels risk having the parts dissolve in the whole, the vantage point becoming lost in the vision. Unless, that is, one grasps from the outset that they are actually extensions of present conditions rather than forecasts of future ones. Such terrors as perpetrated by teenage werewolves like Alex in *A Clockwork Orange* and the domination of gangs like Hell's Angels are near-mild "happenings" placed cheek by jowl with current youth revolutions. And if the prime target of *The Wanting Seed*—overpopulation—is not yet, technically, a *fait accompli,* its proliferating literature, written not by hysterical Cassandras but by sound demographers, attests less to its imminence than, failing a cracking good holocaust, its inevitability.

One, then, must zero in on the contemporaneity of Burgess's issues —something that the ingenious superstructures and novelistic devices often impede. Take as an example the style of both novels. The ferocious and coarse, partly archaic, partly mod, neologic "nadsat" of *A Clockwork Orange* captures perfectly the violence and pace of incidents, breaking down into standard English only when the hero is being brainwashed and stripped of individuality. Clearly, it is always an amazing feat to have the

From *The Consolations of Ambiguity: An Essay on the Novels of Anthony Burgess.* © 1971 by the Curators of the University of Missouri. University of Missouri Press, 1971.

language of a novel not simply *match* the action, but *be* the action. Clearly, too, one quickly wearies of the innovative, especially in matters of an *outré* style that so dazzles readers as to its form that they are almost eager to overlook its content. The brevity of *A Clockwork Orange* probably accounts for the success of its linguistic excess. Burgess, at any rate, has more luck in overplaying his hand in language than in standing pat. Though he was undoubtedly after a much different effect in *The Wanting Seed*, the contrast between the scrupulous impersonality of a Defoe-like, third-person narrator and the nightmarish, surrealistic scenes never quite catches the tone of savagery that the satire seems to be striving for.

Again, there is the matter of structure. The triunal division of *A Clockwork Orange* — Alex damned, Alex purged, Alex resurrected — can be taken, depending on one's predilections at the start, as the falling-rising pattern of comedy or the rising-falling pattern of tragedy. That one may have it either way means, of course, there is a danger in having it neither. If the mode of a novel should say something about its meaning, or at least carry us forward so we may debate it, then we might have wished for a less open-ended conclusion, one that defined as well as disturbed. I find a similar falling off into diffuseness or blurriness in *The Wanting Seed*, in which Burgess, alternating the lives of Tristram and Beatrice-Joanna Foxe, attempts to match the "Pelagian-Augustinian" phases of ebb and flow that symbolize the arbitrary movement of historic cycles. Yet while the reunion of Tristram and Beatrice has been logically anticipated throughout, the pat, almost cliché ending of husband and wife rejoined, coerced no more by the forces of man and nature but rising above them — transfixed, as it were, in the still point of the ineluctable cycle — strikes me as an alogical apotheosis of the human spirit.

Yet both books conclude on notes of "joy": Alex fondling his "britva" as he anticipates the chorale of Beethoven's Ninth and more throat cutting; the Foxes (Adam and Eve and twin offspring?) standing in their Valéry-like "graveyard by the sea," facing the ocean out of which new life will come (*il faut tenter vivre*). The individual is thus endowed with regenerative powers never clearly woven into the fabric of the fiction, and Burgess barters even tentative answers for impressive technique. I feel, in short, that his adroit shock tactics with plot and language, expertise with satire, and partiality to apocalypse — all enviable attributes and potential pluses normally — come dangerously close here to outflanking the substantive ideas. Done as these novels are, with immense energy and cleverness, their sheer "physicalness" all but crushes their metaphysics.

That is a loss, for Burgess has much to tell us. However arbitrary the premises of these novels, however suspect their "political science," their speculations on freedom and free will are frighteningly pertinent. Violently opposing the sterile, mechanical life under totalitarianism, they point no less to the degeneration under anarchy and, further, offer no viable alternative. Freedom stifled is no less opprobrious than freedom unlicensed, but the middle ground — what every liberal imagines is the just and workable compromise — is accounted equally suspect. Burgess has given us in the earlier set of novels a smug, self-satisfied, socialized England that has run down. Too much freedom creates the mess only stability can correct; of course, stability involves the surrender of freedom. Like those of Orwell and Huxley, Burgess's exaggerated portraits of the confrontation between individual and state will ever mystify — until too late — the addled sensibilities who, drugged by the present moment, will neither care about nor comprehend the moment beyond. Even more frightening, we have since Orwell and Huxley moved closer to the impasse where the problems at last overwhelm the solutions, and what we are left with for solution is perhaps only continual re-examination of the problem. Is it not, therefore, a trifle absurd to ponder tortuous issues of mind and soul when daily it grows impossible to cope with external realities like pollution, famine, and overpopulation? Can we even talk of freedom or free will to states that have written them off as mere philosophical aberrations? Yet what meaning can existence have without the continuing quest to define it?

On the one hand, Burgess answers these paradoxes through the nineteenth-century existentialism of writers like Dostoyevski, Nietzsche, and Kierkegaard who dealt with freedom and free will, not in historic, but in metaphysical contexts. If revolution and the state initiated a new order of debate on freedom versus authority — from which arose the issue of free will — then the problems were quickly desocialized thereafter. Libertarianism became as much the immovable force as necessitarianism the impenetrable object. Indeed, the best synthesis of the weird symbiosis between free will and freedom is still to be found in Ivan Karamazov's proem on the Grand Inquisitor, which, wrenched from its place in the novel, can satisfy radical and reactionary alike. Man, weak and imperfect as he is, can never bear the loneliness of living absolutely by free will and so surrenders the ideal of freedom to the *Realpolitik* of society. As Dostoyevski realized all too sadly and well, most of us, lacking the superhuman inner strength necessary to do otherwise, submit our wills to Pilates and Inquisitors, rather than exercise them in an imitation of Christ.

Burgess's approach within this convention explains some of the broader outlines of both novels—especially since his hypothetical states dog the heels of totalitarian regimes. But clearly the Europe of a hundred years ago is not the "global village" of today. The revolutionary spirit abroad in the nineteenth century may have accounted in great part for its philosophy, but the trend of states toward a finer and fiercer repression (with no exit in sight) created an entirely new metaphysics on the older issues. Today, though man has more freedom to discuss his powers of freedom, the ugly fact is that the opportunities for demonstrating it have become more and more narrow. Striking out in acts of violence against the state that usurps freedom only binds our wills more rigorously to the state. Enigmatically, violence is not a display of free will at all, but an echo of historic determinism. For whether we like it or not, we cannot exercise free will in a vacuum; and though we like it less and less, the state is still the "objective correlative" for the freedom we seek. The true problem, in other words, is no longer how one learns to love Big Brother, nor what happens when one does not, but what results from not caring one way or the other about him.

What is chilling about *A Clockwork Orange* and *The Wanting Seed* is not so much Burgess's awareness of these philosophic questions, but the dead ends to which the empiricism of his answers leads. He achieves a partial perspective in *The Wanting Seed* in pirating from the Pelagian-Augustinian tussle over free will in order to superimpose metaphysics on history. His ENSPUN, a future conglomerate of English states, moves by fits and starts according to "theologico-mythical concepts" of two historic cycles that alternately place man in one phase or the other.

> "Pelagius [as Tristram Foxe tells his history class] denied the doctrine of Original Sin and said that man was capable of working out his own salvation. . . . All this suggests human perfectibility. Pelagianism was thus seen to be at the heart of liberalism and its derived doctrines, especially Socialism and Communism. . . . Augustine, on the other hand, had insisted on man's inherent sinfulness and the need for the redemption through divine grace. This was seen to be at the bottom of Conservatism and other *laissez-faire* and non-progressive political beliefs. . . . The opposed thesis, you see. . . . The whole thing is quite simple, really."

This exposition comes early on and *is* "quite simple"—that is, if one contents himself with surfaces. I mentioned above that this philosophic rationale provides the structure for the novel. It also supplies the several antipodal outlooks (the optimistic and pessimistic, borne respectively by Beatrice-Joanna and Tristram) and accounts for the crucial rationalistic and voluntaristic arguments over the individual and the state (the Pelagian would allow man freedom of choice to populate himself out of existence; the Augustinian would stifle his natural instincts and freedom in order to preserve the state). Finally, in the most clever of ways, the rationale parallels the lineal development of the protagonists as their lives crisscross in the alternating historic cycles.

But what is also "quite simple" to ignore are the modern ironies Burgess twists into the debate between the venerable bishop-saint and the heretic monk. Augustine and Pelagius clashed, one may remember, over the most fundamental issues relating to free will: original sin and divine grace. Augustine developed the theory that Adam's sin is transmitted from parents to children throughout all generations through the sexual act (which, inevitably accompanied by lust, is sinful), while Pelagius taught that sin originates in man's following the bad example of Adam and that it is continued in mankind by force of habit. Consequently, Augustine concluded that man's ultimate salvation resided in the divine grace of God alone; Pelagius argued—with something approaching psychological insight—that divine grace is bestowed according to merit and that man, in the exercise of his free and morally responsible will, will take the determining initiative in matters of salvation.

This is very solemn stuff, and I hope the reader will not lose patience with me when I say that much of it is beside Burgess's main point, though very ingeniously tangential to it. As Tristram pedantically remarks, "The theology subsisting in our opposed doctrines of Pelagianism and Augustinianism has no longer any validity. We use these mythical symbols because they are peculiarly suited to our age, an age relying more and more on the perceptual, the pictorial, the pictographic." But translated into modern historic terminology, the theology has an added force, albeit an inverted one. The concept of original sin, the theory, is positively silly and insignificant when placed beside the desperate reality of overpopulation accruing from lust, fornication, and marriage. Birth is accountable for both the theological and historical problem as well as for the metaphysical bind of the protagonists. And, by the same token, one cannot even quixotically imagine that God's grace will clear up the population explosion; it is to God's modern counterpart, the state, that one looks for salvation.

A diagram of these three operative levels in *The Wanting Seed* might look something like this:

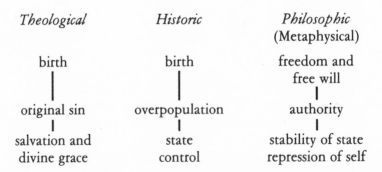

Theological	*Historic*	*Philosophic* (Metaphysical)
birth	birth	freedom and free will
original sin	overpopulation	authority
salvation and divine grace	state control	stability of state repression of self

It would be absurd to suggest that the novel reduces to so pat a ratio, but I hope the schematic illustrates fairly how Burgess empirically handles the abstractions such a book raises. The fact is that *The Wanting Seed*, exposing the Pelagian and Augustinian views of man, carries us through both sieges of the historic cycle: one, when man lives unnaturally (sterilized, controlled, advanced for homosexuality and abstinence, a utilitarian being stabilized by the state); the other, in which he has degenerated to almost "total depravity" — blood lust, cannibalism, pagan fertility rites — anarchic but free.

The Wanting Seed, an anabasis of two protagonists bent on quite different quests into the "interior," clearly expostulates the choice between salvation through stability and control or damnation through unlimited freedom — with little hope left for the human race no matter what the chosen alternative. To believe in preserving at all costs our birthright, despite the inevitable disaster of its course, is to see the "changeling" Beatrice-Joanna (adrift in the madhouse of a world) as a heroine of natural functions. Yet, to uncover with Tristram — seeking his betrayed Isolde — the cruelty and savagery and desperation behind biological urges and primitive instincts is to negate whatever sanctified mystique may once have attended parturition among civilized man. Eight years ago when Burgess wrote the novel he seemed something of an alarmist; today, I fear, the book appears in some ways almost a conservative document. Prophetic though it be, and as strongly as the impact of its dilemmas and paradoxes are felt, there is a slight aura of approbation hovering about that eternal, instinctual, animal act we so vacantly ennoble. Probably not until the very word *birth* — sentimental, charismatic — is purged from the language and *breeding* substituted will our sensibilities become attuned to how mindless and automatic the beginning of life is, yet how complex and hopeless the conditions when too many beginnings may truly mean our end.

I have not meant in all of this to sound canting. One cannot really improve on *The Wanting Seed* as Burgess wrote it. It is harsh, terrifying, exciting in its thorough pointing up of man's potential for total depravity as either slave or rebel and of the depravity of the state as well. Like all good satirists, Burgess lashes out with savage indignation at stupidity and blind error and lacerates our disastrous pretensions at solving human problems at the expense of human beings. For that reason I feel a certain exasperation at his consigning everything to the crucible of time. I am appalled at the final close-up of a heroine who has brought gurgling twins into an overpopulated world. I am not comforted — however confident the thalassographers — at the thought of reaping gifts from the sea after we have raised hell with the rest of the earth. (That Beatrice-Joanna and Tristram are finally united near the sea is perhaps a bit too mechanical, in view of "Pelagius" and the English equivalent of his name, "Morgan," meaning "man of the sea.") And I positively reject Burgess's notion of our starting anew the cycle of human perfectibility (the "Pelphase") when so little in the novel has demonstrated our capabilities for it. I balk, in short, at being led to the threshold of some revelation and not being taken across.

In a way, the novel reminds me of the fairy tale in which a dedicated and decidedly indefatigable sister knits shirts for her brothers who have been transformed into swans. She must, one may remember, complete her work by an appointed time, and in the few moments during the day when her brothers revert to human form throw the garments over them. When the deadline arrives she has all but the sleeve of one shirt ready, and the youngest brother, on whom it falls, lives encumbered thereafter with a wing.

In *The Wanting Seed* Burgess smothers us in the mantle of Augustinian guilt, leaving the smallest of rents through which the Pelagian ideal must intrude itself. It is something like hope, but equally a thing with feathers. Though one sympathizes with the practical difficulties of a writer who is working himself out of metaphysical corners, one remains conscious that hope, such as we have come to understand it in the novel, is illusive, impractical, unsound, and insubstantial. We cannot, of course, stop hoping; it is one of the few things left us. But once the state, bent exclusively on its own survival, has defected from any humanistic response to psychological needs and substitutes instead order, stability, materialism, and technocracy, even the hypothetical chances for hope seem not only tenuous but nil.

I seriously doubt whether governmental structure and strictures as we now know them can further the *rapprochement* between the political and human ideal—so long, that is, as "polidicy" is everywhere evoked to justify the ways of the state to man the justification is built on self-perpetuating mutual suspicion and propped by foundering abstractions. Philosophically, I think, the issue—perhaps the only issue—still remains that of freedom and free will. The state distrusts man because he leaves everything to choice; man, the state, because it leaves nothing to it. The seed truly wanting in both is the seed of goodness from which, possibly, the "golden age" will germinate. But when the genesis of "good" people like Beatrice-Joanna and Tristram are aborted, when man is no longer allowed to choose between goodness and its necessary correspondent evil, when the seed withers on those drier, ethical grounds of right and wrong, then human perfectibility has not the remotest chance of being realized.

Much of this becomes explicit in A Clockwork Orange, though the raison d'être of Burgess's rawest, grimmest, most famous novel can be found toward the end of The Wanting Seed when Tristram hopefully asks the War Office major: "Do you think people are fundamentally good?" And the officer replies: "Well . . . they now have a chance to be good." Those skeptical of the chances governments afford us will find A Clockwork Orange sustaining to such skepticism. It is a book focusing on "the chance to be good" and proceeding from a single, significant existential dilemma: Is an evil human being with free choice preferable to a good zombie without it? Indeed, at two points in the novel Burgess spells out the dilemma for us. On one occasion, Alex, about to submit to conditioning, is admonished by the prison chaplain:

> "It may not be nice to be good, little 6655321. It may be horrible to be good. . . . Does God want goodness or the choice of goodness? Is a man who chooses the bad perhaps in some ways better than a man who has the good imposed upon him? . . . A terrible terrible thing to consider. And yet, in a sense, in choosing to be deprived of the ability to make an ethical choice, you have in a sense really chosen the good."

And on the other, the unwitting F. Alexander, with whom Alex finds sanctuary temporarily, similarly remarks:

> "You've sinned, I suppose, but your punishment has been out of all proportion. They have turned you into something other than a human being. You have no power of choice any longer. You are committed to socially acceptable acts, a little machine capable only of good. . . . But the essential intention is the real sin. A man who cannot choose ceases to be a man."

Yet, were this all Burgess had to say on the matter, the impetus of the dilemma would lose substantially in force. Society at large has never troubled itself with the existential agony (unless to repress some manifestation of it), and judging from the preponderance of sentiment abroad today, it would undoubtedly applaud the conditioning process that champions stability over freedom. But Burgess has found inhering in the central dilemma considerations even more immediate. What distinctions between good and evil are possible in the contemporary world? As absolutes, have such distinctions not been totally perverted or obliterated? And as relative terms, depending for definition on what each negates or excludes, have they not become purely subjective? In a technically perfect society that has sapped our vitality for constructive choice, we are, whether choosing good or evil, zombies of one sort or another: Each of us is a little clockwork orange making up the whole of one great clockwork orange.

I am not suggesting that this spare masterpiece necessarily answers the questions it raises. Even a philosophic novel is fiction before philosophy, a fact too easily lost sight of in the heat of critical exuberance. If anything, Burgess sharpens our sensibilities, shapes our awareness of his main arguments, by letting us see the extent to which the human quotient dwindles in the face of philosophic divisions. One must, therefore, reject equally any monistic or dualistic readings of the novel, not because the book, per se, is complex, but because the issues are. It is obviously impossible to resolve syllogistically which is the greater evil perpetrated in *A Clockwork Orange:* Alex's rape and murder or the state's conditioning of his mind and, as some would have it, soul. Passive goodness and dynamic evil are choices that in themselves may or may not be acceptable or unacceptable, but that in terms of the novel are neither. My own preference is to view the book pluralistically, to see it as a kind of varieties of existential experience, involving at every turn mixtures of both good and evil that move outward through widening concentric circles of choice from the esthetic (ugliness, beauty) to the moral (sin, redemption). And, as with *The Wanting Seed,* the experiences are empirically stated.

Let me start with the esthetic that is oddly integral to the novel — its language. *Vesch* and *tolchock* and *smeck* and about 250 other nadsat neologisms characterize Alex's era as distinctively as *phony* and *crap* do Holden Caulfield's. Whatever sources Burgess drew upon ("Odd bits of old rhyming slang. . . . A bit of gypsy talk, too. But most of the roots are Slav. Propaganda. Subliminal penetration."), it has generally been the brutality, harshness, distortion, artificiality, and synthetic quality of the coinages that have fascinated those (myself included) who make the

direct connection between the way Alex speaks and how he acts. The language is all of this — an "objective correlative" with a vengeance — but it is
something more. Burgess is also a musician, and any passage of sustained
nadsat reflects certain rhythms and textures and syncopations. As the
following:

> Oh, it was gorgeosity and yumyumyum. When it came to the
> Scherzo I could viddy myself very clear running and running
> on like very light and mysterious nogas, carving the whole litso
> of the creeching world with my cutthroat britva. And there
> was the slow movement and the lovely last singing movement
> still to come. I was cured all right.

In its simplicity and naturalness as well as its wholeness and continuity, this final paragraph of *A Clockwork Orange* sings to me much as
those freewheeling lapses in Molly Bloom's soliloquy. It is hardly coincidental that Alex's favorite piece of music is Beethoven's Ninth, rich in
dissonances that only the professional ear can detect, but filled also with
as many untapped, infinite (so it seems) harmonies. In a way it is easy to
understand why musical conservatives of Beethoven's time could find the
Ninth "ugly" by the then rigorous harmonic standards and why, as a matter of fact, more than one critic fled from the concert hall at the beginning of the "lovely last singing movement." Alex's language is, in its way,
ugly, too; but place it alongside the bland and vapid professional or
everyday language of the doctors and warders and chaplains and hear how
hollow their language rings. Burgess was out to show how sterile and
devitalized language could become without a continuing dynamics
behind it; how, in fact, the juice had been squeezed from it; and how,
contrarily, Alex emerges as something of a poet, singing dithyrambs to
violence, but revealing through the terrifying beauty of his speech the
naked beauty of an uninhibited psyche.

The choice of an esthetic substantiates the several existential modes
without explaining how the maladjustment — itself an indication of social,
psychological, and biological "evils" — came about. The causes are naturally grounded in current events, and Burgess has spelled them out in
earlier writings. Alex, the gross product of welfare state overkill, is not
"depraved because he is deprived" but because he is indulged. "Myself,"
he notes rather pathetically at the beginning of *A Clockwork Orange*, "I
couldn't help a bit of disappointment at things as they were those days.
Nothing to fight against really. Everything as easy as kiss-my-sharries."
Alex's utopia is more than the result of suprapermissiveness and self-
gratification; it is the consequence of the "original sin" inborn with every

offspring of modern organizational leviathans. Having discovered that existence has always meant freedom, but never having been taught "goodness," Alex responds predictably and inevitably to the killing burden of choice.

Socially, he and his "droogs" parody the formless, shadowy, omnipotent political entity that sports with them as they with "lewdies." This Kafkaesque infinite regression is frightening enough, though I find even more so Burgess's repeated inferences that we are all, in some way or another, products of conditioning: tools to be manipulated and clockwork oranges whether we will or no. Alex, not unlike Meursault or K. or — as Burgess more slyly than reasonably lets us imagine — Christ, is the mere scapegoat. He is the one called upon to expiate for the existence of others because he has dared question — or (in this case) has been forced to question — his own.

I don't know that Burgess offers any clear-cut expansion of the psychological and biological evils of modern life, but he does dramatize with vitality the theory that we are by now — depending on our luck — either neurotic or paranoid. Alex's particular routine sado-masochism — nightly orgies of "tolchocking" and the old "in-out in-out," alternating between sabbaticals at the all-too-Freudian Korova Milkbar and withdrawals (onanistic and otherwise) into his multi-speakered stereo womb — may be the healthy neurosis standing between Alex and the paranoia of the populace, though it proves something of a disaster for those elected as outlets for his self-expression. Yet more insidious is the growing feeling one gets in reading A Clockwork Orange of governments encouraging violence in order to whip up and feed the paranoia that will ultimately engender allegiance through fear. Ironically, Alex, on the surface at least, is less psychologically distorted and biologically frustrated in his career of violence than those he terrorizes or those who seek to condition him. And, in a more significant way, his small-scale brutalities reflect no deeper abnormality than those of larger scale perfected by the engineers of power politics.

Alex, of course, does not intellectualize his *Non serviam*. For one thing, he wouldn't know how to; for another, there is no need to. The evils of intellect — ignorance and error — have brought the state to a point at which only the fruits of escalated intellectual achievement can check and contain (if that is now the sole function left the state!) the robots it has brought into being. Nothing is mystifying about our present disenchantment with intellectuals who, however motivated or why, have skillfully and near totally excised with their finely honed organizations, systems, and machines the last vestiges of our intuition. Burgess makes a case for the Alex-breed being one of the last, though obviously not impregnable, strongholds of intuition. Yet Alex is neither a purely feeling (if ignoble) savage nor a crusader warring against thought. He is a prototype of those who, muddling means and ends by lumping them together, rebel out of a studied defiance to intellect, rather than out of any untutored intuitive urge. Intellect having failed to show them the "truth that shall make men free," intuition alone must sustain the illusion of freedom and itself become accepted as the creative act or be confused with it. Such intuitional virtues seem to account for Alex's successful "dratsing" with Georgie and Dim:

> When we got into the street I viddied that thinking is for the gloopy ones and that the oomny ones use like inspiration and what Bog sends. For now it was lovely music that came to my aid. There was an auto ittying by and it had its radio on, and I could just slooshy a bar or so of Ludwig van (it was the Violin Concerto, last movement), and I viddied right at once what to do.

What Alex does is carve up both of them a bit with his "britva," yet the episode is more significant in retrospect than in context. Alex's *natural* reflex of elation in the face of violence — inspired here by Beethoven — later becomes a *conditioned* reflex against violence after his bout with the "Ludovico technique," a name, I imagine, not chosen at random by Burgess. The distortion of intellect and intuition leads to an unresolvable Manicheanism: What are we, where are we when we can be programmed into calling evil what is so clearly the "good and beautiful?" In a clockwork-orange society we may as well surrender any pretense for distinguishing between good and evil; when we call them by the identical name we know we have been brainwashed past hope. In this respect, *A Clockwork Orange* shows refinements even beyond *1984*. Winston Smith, having undergone physical tortures on a par with primitive atrocities and unrelenting mental cruelties predicated on external fears, quite naturally betrays the woman he loves and learns to love Big Brother. But Alex, robbed of his will, reduced to an automaton, taught to be sickened by violence, is made "good" only by killing in him what was already *the* good.

Both Winston and Alex "die" when they can no longer love. Yet, if *1984* is grimly conclusive in showing the death of a mind and heart at the hands of the state, *A Clockwork Orange* is equally effective in questioning the finality of the death. Burgess brings in (not for shock tactics alone) one of the original archetypes through which Alex finds salvation: the fall, or in this case, the jump. His attempted suicide is, according to Christian dogma, a transgression against God's will, grace, and judgment, and, existentially, the inexcusable surrender of human freedom. Alex, in other words, has been half-dragged, half-propelled down paths of problematical and actual evil to arrive at the lethal nadir of moral evil: sin. And having plumbed the depths, he can only rise. He is a slave to fate rather than choice (the things that happen to him in the last third of the book recapitulate those he initiated in the first third), a victim (no longer victimizer) without refuge, unsuited for Christ-like martyrdom ("If that veck had stayed I might even have like presented the other cheek"), physically coming apart at the seams and mentally wracked. From this condition, his try at "snuffing it" becomes the last desperate exertion of a murdered will and, paradoxically, the means to its resurrection.

Despite the unanswerable paradoxes and dilemmas of *A Clockwork Orange*, which remain unaltered in the ambiguity of its conclusion, my own notions as to the book's ultimate intent are perhaps slightly more irreverent than ambivalent. I cannot escape the idea that Burgess has intended Alex's sickness—the *nausée* lodged in nonchoice—to symbolize a new concept of *Angst* neatly antithetical to Kierkegaard's "sickness unto death," the "fear and trembling" accruing from the infinite possibilities of choice. And, further, I suspect Alex's jump, the fall by which he is redeemed (the resulting concussion undoes his conditioning), in some way approximates the Kierkegaardian "leap into faith": the intuitive passage from doubt to faith after the cold logic of intellect fails. Alex has done wrong, been evil, sinned, but all as preparation for his redemption. The faith he finds is a specimen of love, joy, freedom. Ironically, he must leave HOME in order to reach it in the same way a man must "lose his life [before] he save it." And his cure is both of the body and soul. "It was," says Alex, "like as though to get better I had to get worse." Burgess seems to be saying that, in a brutal, resigned, mechanical world—a world turned clockwork—love must come from hate, good from evil, peace from violence, and redemption from sin.

How? Unfortunately there are no panaceas for metaphysical or existential ills, and Burgess is not a prescriptive writer anyway. Human problems are inexhaustible so long as there are human beings; eradicate one and you eradicate the other. Short of that, one might find the answer to *A Clockwork Orange* in *The Wanting Seed*—and vice versa, but I very much doubt that either solution would serve for long. Give man unlimited choice? He will make a botch of it. Deprive him of all but the "right" choice? He is no longer a man. The seeds and fruits of freedom, both novels tell us, are bitter, but man is now harvesting only what he has sown.

JOHN J. STINSON

The Manichee World
of Anthony Burgess

Anthony Burgess may possibly not be "England's No. 1 novelist" as he is extravagantly acclaimed on the covers of some of the paperback editions of his novels. Still in all, if his achievement as a novelist were to be judged by the enthusiasm of reviewers and the diversity of laudatory comments received, he would seem to hold a position of strong dominance over most of his contemporaries. The exceptional success that Burgess has enjoyed with reviewers is quite remarkably strange in the light of the fact that his work has been largely ignored by academic critics. This state of neglect has continued to prevail despite the fact that six or seven reviewers, both in this country and in England, have gone out of their way to point this out specifically and to argue for his inclusion within the ranks of the most talented novelists of the present day. This state of critical neglect may very well not obtain long, however, since Burgess, a prolific critic himself, is now in the process of achieving increased scholarly visibility by his critical books and articles. It seems likely too that far more general attention will be brought to Burgess because of Stanley Kubrick's widely acclaimed adaptation of Burgess's novel *A Clockwork Orange*.

It seems to me that there are several probable reasons for the relative critical neglect of Burgess's novels, but the chief of these seems to be that the critics cannot seem to find a "handle" to his novels. This is no surprise, either, since they are widely diverse in subject matter and mode. The phrase that keeps profferring itself as a "key" to Burgess's novels

From *Renascence* 26, no. 1 (Autumn 1973). © 1973 by the Catholic Renascence Society, Inc.

among reviewers seems to be "black comedy." *In vacuo*, however, as it usually is, it does not mean very much. Besides, it is critically suspect. It is dangerously inaccurate, too, if, for example one were to think that Burgess should be classified with John Hawkes, Terry Southern, William Burroughs, J. P. Donleavy, Kurt Vonnegut, or John Barth. "Black comedy" is a relatively meaningless term unless its user defines the philosophy he sees behind it. It can be agreed fairly easily, though, I think, that all black comedy necessarily depends on some radical incongruity in the basic human condition. Burgess's theory and practice of black comedy can probably best be approached through the overt metaphysical-philosophical schemata that he has imposed on nearly all of his novels. His own direct shorthand for denoting the metaphysical-religious view that is at the center of all his novels is to label it Manicheeism. This seems to me a conscious and direct clue to the vision, structure, and effect of each of his novels. The words *Manicheeism* or *Manichee* appear directly in three of the novels; another (*The Wanting Seed*) continually employs the term *Augustinianism,* a close but more orthodox cousin of Manicheeism. It is not easy to sum up Manicheeism in a few words, but it should be said first that this heresy posits as its basic premise a radical dualism. Matter, and hence the body, is base and of the Power of Darkness; it is the source of the evil present in the world. Only Spirit is good and comes from God. While it was the firm duty of every believer of the Manichean Church to strive for the Light, the spiritual, and thus, ideally, to lead rigidly ascetic lives, it was recognized that there was a nearly hopeless intermixture of Light and Dark elements in this earth. The larger, looser, more encompassing meaning of the word *Manichean,* then, came to signify any of various dualistic beliefs that viewed evil as a positive agency emanating from a power coequal with the Power of Good. To know either one of these powers was, by opposition, to know something of the other. The interpenetration of good and evil is one of Burgess's main themes, as it is also for Graham Greene, one of the chief influences upon Burgess.

Sharply conflictive opposites, polarities, antinomies, and dualisms have served countless novelists (to say nothing, of course, of dramatists) as both organizing center and life-view. Some names spring instantaneously to mind—Hawthorne, Conrad, Mann. It is relatively easy to understand their useful employment in Hawthorne, for example, since he is writing allegory (or psychological parable), but it is far more difficult to make sense of their employment as organizational center in the social / metaphysical satires of Burgess. But, to use words which are very nearly Burgess's own, out of conflict must come some artistic confluence: it is

precisely the vision of unity which is what "the artist sells." The confluence in Burgess can best begin to be found in those passages which adum-
brate the human dichotomy in Manichean terms:

> Ennis had become a Manichee, at home in a world of per-
> petual war. It did not matter what the flags or badges were; he
> looked only for the essential opposition — Wet and Dry, Left
> Hand and Right Hand, Yin Yang, X and Y. Here was the
> inevitable impasse, the eternal stalemate.

> "Russia," said the Doctor, ruminatively. "I think we must go
> on, Madox and I. Towards the East. I am tired of categories, of
> divisions, of opposites. Good, evil; male, female; positive,
> negative. That they interpenetrate is no real palliative, no
> ointment for the cut. What I seek is the *continuum*, the merg-
> ing, Europe is all Manichees: Russia has become the most
> European of them all."

These quotes from *A Vision of Battlements* and *Honey for the Bears*
demonstrate the surprisingly perceptive awareness that many of Burgess's
characters have of their own Manichean tendencies. A study of the psychological and mental constitution of each of these characters will reveal
that their Manichean tendencies have the same impulse as that which
gave life to the heretical religion of the early Middle Ages itself: the attempt to explain the nature of evil in the world in terms that were intellectually convincing and psychologically satisfying. Already, then, it
should become clear that we are approaching both the well-springs of
religion and of tragedy.

It is with legitimate hesitancy, though, that one would say that
Burgess is a "religious" writer, even in the same sense that one would say
it of his contemporary William Golding. But Burgess himself has made
one illuminating and prominently placed comment on the possibilities of
the contemporary religious novel. In a signed front-page article in *The
Times Literary Supplement* (March 3, 1966), entitled significantly
enough "The Manicheans," Burgess treats of the difficulties of subsum-
ing art to specifically religious ends. About the novel he says the following:

> Of all the arts, that of the novel least excites ecstatic twinges; it
> pursues formal beauty with less enthusiasm than either music
> or poetry. This is because it is more committed to the represen-
> tation of life, and life is always eager to disrupt pattern. But
> religion is a part of life, and — since here lies an opportunity to

invest plain fiction with refractions of the supernatural, lifting
the reader's heart as though he were listening to music — one
would expect religious experience to provide more of the
novelist's subject-matter than it actually does. I do not mean
the tribulations of priests among the poor, or deanery gossip,
or preordination doubts; I mean rather the imaginative analysis of themes like sainthood, behaviour, even that dangerous
beatific vision.

If we should expect that Evelyn Waugh and, far more particularly,
Graham Greene are prominent in Burgess's mind at this point, we are
soon proven right — he devotes lengthy paragraphs to both Greene and
Waugh. Of course, there are not today very many genuinely competent
novelists who are writing religious novels, and this is the chief point
Burgess makes in the article. The other writers he mentions as "religious"
writers are all English (apparently Burgess did not have enough space to
get into the "cosmic themes" of the American novel as essentially religious). These are William Golding, Iris Murdoch, Angus Wilson, Muriel
Spark, and even Kingsley Amis whose *One Fat Englishman* Burgess reads
as "an allegory of the Seven Deadly Sins." Burgess modestly does not
mention his own novels, but the tenor and direction of the whole article
imply that the novelist has a duty to be concerned with so fundamental
and meaningful a fact of human experience as religion but that he must
not be misled into using his fiction as a vehicle for a narrowly religious
end.

    While still not mentioning his own fiction, Burgess does, in the
same article, provide a very important remark about the Manichean element in his own novels — although he is speaking of the religious novelist
generally: "There is something in the novelist's vocation which predis-
poses him to a kind of Manicheeism. What the religious novelist often
seems to be saying is that evil is a kind of good, since it is an aspect of the
Ultimate Reality; though what he is really saying is that evil is more interesting to write about than good."

    The phrase "predisposition toward Manicheeism," used in direct ap-
plication to Burgess's novels, tells us very little about their real content
and nothing at all about the motive force behind them — it would be preposterous for us to suppose that Burgess is proselytizing for Manicheeism.
It is informative for what it indicates about the form and technique of the
novels, for how it provides a basis for understanding Burgess's black
humor, his characteristic mode of distortion.

It is, to use Burgess's own term, his "Manichean" vision that gives direct rise to his black humor, or perhaps to be more accurate, we might better say, to his various forms of the grotesque. The true grotesque vision sees the position of man in the universe as radically incongruous. Given hints and longings of immortality, man must live in an organism that he realizes all too painfully is finite. Able as a thinking creature to form a concept of perfection, man is only too aware that he lives in a radically imperfect world. Drawn by intellectual conviction to the moral and the good, man finds that the weaknesses of the flesh lead him time and again to the immoral and the evil. Driven by the dictates of intellect to order his existence, man realizes with exquisite pain that chance frequently rules his life: he feels the fact of Disorder and Chaos more often than that of Design. Man lives in a tantalizingly intermediate state from which the only escape is death. Needless to say, these metaphysical antitheses are, in some deeper sense, at the bases of all art, but for the artist of the grotesque they are poignantly immediate facts of metaphysical experience to be represented in art by the symbolically exaggerated distortion of the everyday world. This Burgess has done throughout his whole novelistic career, although the grotesque elements in his work are not as clearly seen as those of Barth, Hawkes, or Heller, let us say, since in Burgess they are artistically mixed with strong strands of social satire and farce. Ever conscious of the dualities of human experience Burgess, "predisposed to Manicheeism," as he says, will represent them in art. The forms and techniques of this representation at least are grotesque, and it can be said with fairness, I think, that the real core of meaning resides also in the grotesque vision, so that it can only be said in a broader and looser sense of the word that the novels are religious. Burgess does not see an absurd universe, but he does see a grotesque world.

Grotesque in Burgess assumes two chief forms: what may, somewhat arbitrarily, be called "violent grotesque" and "absurd grotesque." Among American writers there have been numerous practitioners of both forms; in many writers the two coexist. There is a general separation of the two forms in Burgess — grotesque violence frequently is used to point up metaphysical incongruity, while grotesque absurdity is frequently reserved for the collective insanities of men living in society.

The violent grotesque is well exemplified in what is probably Burgess's best-known novel, *A Clockwork Orange*. This is one of Burgess's two anti-Utopian novels (the other is *The Wanting Seed*). Set in what seems to be England of the very near future, a nation tottering precariously between the random anarchy of barbarically violent juvenile gangs and a

harshly repressive totalitarian state, the novel has as protagonist and narrator a fifteen-year-old gang leader who, halfway through the narrative,
falls into the clutches of the state. Alex, this warped but not altogether
unintelligent young tough, recounts with relish and a delicious savoring
of detail how he and his "droogies" [gangmates] perpetrated various
atrocious assaults: an old man returning from the library of an evening is
insulted and assaulted; his false teeth are ripped cruelly from his mouth
and crunched by the stomps of the teens' heavy boots; heavy ringed
knuckles slam into his bared gums until his mouth is a riot of red; he is
stripped and kicked for good measure. And this is only the very beginning of violence that exceeds de Sade in intensity of not imaginativeness.
Storekeepers, husband and wife, are brutally beaten and robbed; a wife is
savagely gang raped in her own invaded home as her husband is forced to
watch helplessly; two pubescent girls of ten are raped screaming; an old
lady, a wealthy recluse, meets her death trying to defend herelf and her
valuables during a robbery. And all this plenty—and more—is accomplished by Alex and his three gangmates on the two consecutive days
that comprise part 1, seventy-four pages of the novel.

All this violence is meant to shock, and repulse, and of course it
does. But, given such a summary one would be immediately dubious
about the possibility of any artistic effect: he would wonder whether this
was not either the worst sort of sensationalism, or else psychological shock
therapy working to produce an immediate emetic effect, and subsequently to provoke the reader to take rather direct social action of some
sort. But the novel is neither sadistic pandering nor propaganda; it is
most definitely not kinetic pseudo-art. *A Clockwork Orange* alone very
nearly reveals Burgess as a master technician of the grotesque.

The writer who utilizes the violent grotesque as a technique of his art
must be careful that the violence never get out of control and become an
end, pure and simple, in itself. If it does it will only repel and nauseate.
The novel *in toto* must somehow succeed in conveying to the reader (consciously or subconsciously, more preferably the latter) that the violence is
but a metaphor for contingent possibility on either the metaphysical or
social plane. The reader must be brought to feel with the force of conviction that existentially or socially things are in some way markedly out of
tilt for man. (This, of course, can be handled in such a way that it is pro-
ductive of nausea at the very well of being, but it should not be the instant wretch of disgust brought by sadistic rot.)

Burgess's awesome black comic craft is testified to in *A Clockwork
Orange* by the fact that we can approach the vicious assault on an old man

or the murder of an old lady with lighthearted gaiety, if not joyful mirth. Our feelings come to have the ambivalence that they ultimately do only when our moral reactions, drugged into unwatchfulness, suddenly rouse themselves and come panting up indignantly. But what Burgess has succeeded in doing by the near-miracle of his craft, particularly by his linguistic inventiveness, is temporarily to make us one with the wantonly brutal young assaulters:

> He [the old man returning from the library] looked a malenky bit poogly when he viddied the four of us like that, coming up so quiet and polite and smiling, but he said: "Yes? What is it?" in a very loud teacher-type goloss, as if he was trying to show us he wasn't poogly. . . . "You naughty old veck, you," I said, and then we began to filly about with him. Pete held his rookers and Georgie sort of hooked his rot open for him and Dim yanked out his false zoobies, upper and lower. He threw these down on the pavement and then I treated them to the old boot-crush, though they were hard bastards like, being made of some new horrorshow plastic stuff. The old veck began to make sort of chumbling shooms — "wuf waf wof" — so Georgie let go of holding his goobers apart and just let him have one in the toothless rot with his ringy fist, and that made the old veck start mooning a lot then, then out comes the blood, my brothers, real beautiful. So all we did then was to pull his outer platties off, stripping him down to his vest and long underpants (very starry; Dim smeched his head off near), and then Pete kicks him lovely in his pot, and we let him go.

What forestalls our revulsion at the basically realistic scene of violence (although even more realistically immediate perhaps to the England and America of the 1950s when gang violence was at its height) is the distancing through the use of invented language. Burgess has here freely invented his own teen-age argot (although much of it is cleverly derived from Russian). We are given to suppose that there is an international, popular subculture whose insidious roots, stretching out everywhere, are Russian, although it is just possible too that the ugly encroachment of Russian cultural elements is Burgess's ironically oblique way of casting a satiric eye at creeping Americanism. The important thing here, though, is that the employment of this marvellously evocative, created language casts a strong aura of strangeness of our fixed responses and ordinary moral sensibilities. Then, too, the reader is strongly drawn to Alex, not so much for what he is in himself, but because he is the only character in the book who approaches flesh and blood since he is, in his own words, "our faithful narrator" and "brother." This, of course, is an old novelistic trick; the reader can easily sympathize with anyone who continually tells him about his life and makes him vicariously share it. The reader in the case of *A Clockwork Orange* ideally becomes a sharer with Alex in the making of mayhem. Removed from his point of orientation, he might even surprise in himself some deep, dark streaks of sadism. Burgess, with an artistically earned Christian pessimism that is characteristic of his novelistic vision generally, invites the reader to see the old Adam everywhere. Alex, after his experience of imprisonment and "rehabilitation" (a methodically thorough brainwashing) goes to the library and takes down "the big book or Bible, as it was called, thinking that might give me like comfort . . . but all I found was about smiting seventy times seven and a lot of Jews cursing and tolchocking [striking] each other, and that made me want to sick, too."

The world of *A Clockwork Orange* is one of the deepest Orwellian nightmare mixed with the blackest realistic violence although, as pointed out, the latter is mitigated by the linguistic alchemy. However, there is still no question but that the novel would have been an overly painful one if the author had made concerted attempts to impose a totally firm realistic structure on his dystopia. This he did not do; elements of what can only be called surrealistic technique mix with a basic realism, placing us within an ultra-violent world that is not quite our own. Feelings of physical revulsion and moral unease can in a sense be sublimated through the surrealistic touches. Dropped headlong into a semi-mysterious universe, we cannot obtain our moral bearings at a moment's notice. While *A Clockwork Orange* can in no way be classified as a surrealist novel if we mean by that the authentic surrealism of the French fictional school that took as a point of departure André Breton's Manifesto of Surrealism (concerned more with painting and poetry than with the novel), it can still be noted that what J. H. Matthews says of this type of novel is applicable to *A Clockwork Orange:* "While reading surrealist novels, we have to adjust to unfamiliar moral attitudes. We have to overcome a feeling of alarm or disturbance released in us by the originality of the structural framework of the narrative and by the presence of those who are not characters, acting out a strange destiny in a world that is not quite our own" (*Surrealism and the Novel*). Driving out into the country in a stolen car, just prior to their invasion of a writer's home and the brutal rape of his wife, Alex and his "droogs" continually hear loud clunks as "snarling, toothy" things fall under the headlights of the wildly speeding car. One of these "things" at least is "big"; all "scream" and are "squelched" under the wheels. Returning also, they run over "odd squealing things" all the way. Thus the detailed violence of the rape scene is enclosed by a small framework of nightmarish fantasy, and the rape itself is apprehended not simply as the lurid act which it is, but also as an intuitively felt metaphysical referent for the evil that is in man or the even more primal chaos that cancerously spreads out from the center of the universe. We feel a vague and deep disturbance at the act rather than the simple and righteously correct reaction of nausea we might otherwise expect of ourselves.

The violent grotesque is everywhere part and parcel of Burgess's *Nothing Like the Sun,* a "story of Shakespeare's love-life," as the subtitle reads. Unquestionably a tour de force, this exuberant novel is perhaps at least something slightly more. There is, actually, little more point in patronizing Burgess, than in patronizing one of his masters, Dickens, by saying that art sometimes crept unwittingly in beneath the level of intention. There is art in Burgess as in Dickens, and in Burgess, at least, it is the product of conscious artistry. The grotesque-violence is present in *Nothing Like the Sun* not only to inject marvellous Elizabethan pitch and color, but because it is thematically and tonally consonant with everything else in the novel. Quite simply put, the novel's theme revolves closely around the monumental struggle between flesh and spirit in the man Shakespeare. But this is not to say, of course, that this conflict is a pure and simple one; remembering our Manicheeism we know that things of the body and of the soul are hopelessly mixed in this world: desires of the flesh for example, may be directed into art to produce great triumphs of the human spirit. Burgess's character "WS" (Shakespeare) is excruciatingly racked by the pain of being human, and it is out of his incessantly bursting humanness that his art is created. Burgess presents us with a Hamlet-like figure, a man great in emotion and in intellect, who is vulnerable precisely because of that greatness. In short, "WS" is a magnified embodiment of all that it means to be human; if every man sometimes has clear intimations of the comic, tragic, or grotesque nature of existence, Shakespeare will have them all the more powerfully.

It is the vision of the human dichotomy that informs the whole of *Nothing Like the Sun.* Burgess has striven hard to represent, at extremes, both the animal and spiritual sides of man, incongruous creature of existence. If the novel then is at times incongruous in effect (WS tossing off the great masterpieces of literature in a fury of inspiration amidst violent surroundings in which there are everywhere smashed pates, broken teeth, and tossed chamberpots) and baroque in style (burstingly overinflated Elizabethan language), that is only so much to the good: it demonstrates the point of the black comedy precisely, while, because of the historical distancing, and because we are used to this type of coloration in literature of and about the Elizabethan period, the craft and technique themselves do not jar. Burgess thoroughly convinces the reader that the grotesque world was in Shakespeare's day the world of everyday.

The extravagent descriptions of teeming Elizabethan London found everywhere throughout the novel are evocative of a mood that is central to the novel's purpose; Burgess's form nearly always equals his intention. One is apt not to see this at first, however, since it is difficult to believe that the many descriptive set-pieces, so obviously relished by their author, are included for anything but their own sake. But one should not be misled; what often appear to be patches of exuberant self-indulgence on the part of the author turn out to be highly functional material. The grotesque and the realistic mix shockingly in an account of the public ex-ecution of three criminals at Tyburn Common which is witnessed by WS. Even the horrifically barbaric hanging, drawing, and quartering is but holiday sport and spectacle to those of the populace fortunate enough to be present:

> Of a sudden the noose was tightened; over the momentary in-breathed silence of this crowd the choking desperation of the hanged could clearly be heard. The second assistant pulled the ladder away sharply. The legs dangled a second but the staring eyes still blinked. Here was art, far more exact than WS's own: the hangman approached with his knife, fire in the sunlight, before the neck could crack, ripped downwards from heart to groin in one slash, swiftly changed knife from right to left, then plunged a mottled fist inside the swinging body. The first assistant took the bloody knife from his master and wiped it with care on a clean cloth, the while his eyes were on the ar-tistry of the drawing. The right hand withdrew, dripping, holding up for all to see a heart in its fatty wrappings; then the left arm plunged to reappear all coiled and clotted with en-trails. The crowd cheered; the girl in front of WS leaped and clapped; a child on his father's shoulder thumbsucked, indif-ferent, understanding nothing of all this, the adult world.

La comédie humaine in *Nothing Like the Sun* is everywhere filled with those paradoxes of life that man inherits because of his dual nature. One of the measures of Burgess's success in this novel is that a most significant paradox is tightly enwrapped within the form of the novel itself: Burgess's Elizabethans appear more human precisely because they are represented as more vitally animal. We as readers are made to see the incongruity of their way of life; they did not—they simply lived it and revelled in it in a completely unselfconscious celebration of the life-urge. They are completely whole men; they are not the fragmented selves, the absurd heroes of modern fiction whose world vision is that of what we might call the "pathetic grotesque." The single, most notable, and expected exception to pure instinctual behavior and unselfconscious action within the novel is of course the hero himself, WS. The paradoxes in the man's life are rife as he is presented by Burgess. Success testifies that he knew his age and was in one sense well suited to it; his active life, his total immersion in affairs both of business and of passion seems certainly to confirm this. But in another sense Life itself, which was exemplified in the living in his own age as perhaps in no other, was an instrument of exquisite torture. As Burgess would have it, WS was of his own time and yet not of it altogether. A giant of thought, feeling, and sensibility, WS would have found life in any age painful; he could only find the supercharged life of his own day consummate agony. However, this last statement fails to observe two of the central paradoxes of the novel: WS would have found life unbearable had he allowed himself the indulgence of pure, detached unlimited reflection, but, being a man of blood rather than of choler, he had to live his life as well. For WS, the frustrations of the human paradox were relieved within the action of living, while the actions of his life itself well illustrated that same human paradox.

The basic human paradoxes that are attendant upon man's dual nature are forcefully illustrated in the Burgess canon by a complementary theatricalism of technique that Burgess seams to suggest, plausibly enough in an essay entitled "Dickens Loud and Clear" in his *Urgent Copy*, largely derives from the example of Dickens, symbolist and master of the grotesque. Burgess's manipulation of his reader's emotional responses by a showman's sleight-of-hand and a pitchman's verbal magic are attributable to a large, thought-out design in his novels; there can be no doubt that his theatricality is so pervasively and so essentially a part of his novels, a conscious part of them, that it must be said to be part of his strategic philosophy. In his novels of the violent grotesque, for example, there is frequently a sudden oscillation from one set of emotional effects to their near-opposite: pathos suddenly becomes irony, compassionate humor is transmogrified into loud, hollow, mocking laughter. Then the current is reversed and the process repeats itself. Burgess's superior craftsmanship is testified to precisely by the fact, though, that the reader does not see this as a carnival trick. He sees it for what it is—a semi-symbolic representation of life itself, an endless drama of shifting flux full of ambiguity and paradox. The theatrics are an integrally important part of the ontological drama being acted out before us. And the drama is that of man, intellectual puppet wracked by passion, caught in an uncertain world halfway between good and evil, between light and darkness, the sublime and the grotesque. The vision is Manichean.

The novels of the "violent grotesque" are indeed "Manichean," at least in Burgess's sense of that world. They are not nihilistic or purely absurdist (as the "black comedy" might lead us to suppose), and this is important. While the total form of these novels everywhere demonstrates the incongruity attendant upon man's existence in the world, their thematic centers are not hollow cores of negation. Laughter or disgust at the ridiculous foibles of petty man always modulates into something very close to awe as he indomitably persists in the business of life and being human. We find ourselves, for example, rooting staunchly for Alex, the punk-hero of *A Clockwork Orange* as he redoubtably attempts to resist the "therapy" (a total brainwashing, approaching, in its effects, a lobotomization of evil impulses) inflicted upon him by the totalitarian state in the second half of *A Clockwork Orange.* And we do not dare view Shakespeare in *Nothing Like the Sun* as an absurdly pitiful object even as he makes a fool of himself over his Dark Lady, who in Burgess's novel is a mysterious and inconstant Negress who rewards WS for his efforts by passing on to him a body-wracking venereal disease. Burgess keeps affirming life and all that goes with life. To experience the full limits of human possibility, even to oscillate violently between the poles of one's divided nature in an electrically powerful response to life, is to be most truly human. Dignification and defilement, tragedy and triumph, sublimity and grotesquerie, become very nearly one. The paradoxes spin endlessly round in the orbit of the Manichean universe. Burgess, seemingly an absurdist, comes close at core to being a romantic, and remains thoroughly a Christian.

JEAN E. KENNARD

Anthony Burgess: Double Vision

For Anthony Burgess, as for Joyce, "The artist is a Promethean figure who ends by usurping the place of Zeus." Burgess writes in *Re Joyce:* "The fundamental purpose of any work of art is to impose order on the chaos of life as it comes to us; in imparting a vision of order the artist is doing what the religious teacher also does (this is one of the senses in which truth and beauty are the same thing)." It is not surprising that of twentieth-century fantasy writers Burgess most admires Nabokov and Joyce, because his use of fantasy is for their purposes rather than for the purposes of the post-Existential novelists of number. Burgess, like Joyce, is "a free-thinking fabulist." He needs his reader to be detached and observing, and so he needs fantasy rather than the techniques of realism, but he does not finally alienate his reader.

Burgess, like Joyce, wishes to manipulate "the commonplaces of language into a new medium that should shock the reader into a new awareness." His language has infinite reverberations. The important thing for Burgess is to keep the reader observing the pattern, yet involved, willing to fit the pieces of the jigsaw puzzle together, and then to believe in the picture. He does not take the reader towards nothingness, but towards an image of all-inclusiveness, where "everything is there at once." His purpose, like Joyce's, is the "atonement, at-one-ment, of contradictions." Burgess writes novels of nightmare.

Burgess, one of the most prolific of postwar British writers, is the

---

From *Number and Nightmare: Forms of Fantasy in Contemporary Fiction.*© 1975 by Archon Books, The Shoestring Press, Inc.

author of sixteen novels published under his own name, of two published under the pseudonym Joseph Kell, and of a prodigious amount of criticism, among the best of which is his work on Joyce: *Re Joyce* and *A Shorter Finnegan's Wake*. Although almost all of Burgess's fiction illustrates the same basic philosophic stance, the kinds of fantasy he employs vary considerably. Since it would be impossible [here] to discuss each book in detail, I have chosen the five novels that illustrate most clearly both Burgess's answer to the post-Existential dilemma and his basic method of conveying it: *A Clockwork Orange, The Wanting Seed, Tremor of Intent, Enderby,* and *MF.*

Burgess's novels deal with the same metaphysical questions as those of Heller, Barth, Purdy, and Vonnegut: the purpose of human existence, the nature of identity, the value and significance of language; but his answers—and he, unlike the previous novelists I have discussed [elsewhere], has answers—are not the post-Existential ones. As comments in various interviews and many of his novels indicate, Burgess is directly answering Sartre's and Camus' notion that there is no essential pattern in the universe and that the relationship between man and his universe is therefore irrational.

MF, perhaps, demonstrates most clearly that Burgess is answering the post-Existential view. The protagonist, Miles Faber, believes he can define himself through acts of will, create his own identity in the way Sartre suggests. He imagines he is completely free and seeks for the poems of a little-known writer in whose work he hopes to find "Words and colors totally free because totally meaningless." He learns, however, that "Nobody's free. . . . choice is limited by inbuilt structures." Burgess reveals his interest in Existentialism also in his comments about his novels. For example, in an interview with Thomas Churchill, Burgess has stated that the central theme of *A Clockwork Orange* is "the idea of free will. This is not just half-baked existentialism, it's an old Catholic theme."

If Burgess's answer is the Catholic one—and he says himself that he "will not allow Catholicism to go over to the converts" nor "allow the Protestants to attack it," that what he writes "looks like Catholic writing"—it is certain only some Catholic doctrines interest him. Like Hillier, the hero of his novel *Tremor of Intent,* Burgess seems to have an Augustinian belief in the existence of evil and a sense of "what a bloody Manichean mess life is." Duality is the key to Burgess's view of reality; the essence of reality for him—and there are essences in Burgess's scheme as opposed to Sartre's—is its double nature. "Ultimate reality," says Hillier, "is a dualism or a game for two players." In religious terms this means that good and evil cannot exist without one another, "There is truly evil lying coiled in the good." But as Burgess realizes, "we don't believe in good and evil any more"; we need new terms. Each of the five Burgess novels illustrates this duality in new terms: *A Clockwork Orange* in psychological terms; *The Wanting Seed* in historical/sociological terms; *Tremor of Intent* in political terms; *Enderby* in aesthetic terms; *MF* in terms of the relationship between society's structures and those of language.

The basic method of each Burgess novel is to present the reader with two visions, sometimes two antithetical world views, sometimes two apparently opposed aspects of one personality, and to invite him to make a choice. The choice often proves to be a false one; the two visions are a double vision, a dualism, inseparable parts of the one reality. The true choice lies elsewhere, between this duality and another negative value. The great evil in Burgess's view is to see life as unstructured and therefore capable of being completely controlled by man. The world is not neutral, not simply there. Burgess's use of the double vision is reminiscent of Vonnegut's, but there is an important difference between them. Vonnegut, a novelist of number, allows each vision to undercut the other, leaving the reader with nothing; Burgess, a novelist of nightmare, shows how the two visions are really one, leaving the reader with unity.

In *A Clockwork Orange* Burgess presents a concept of human nature quite different from the Sartrean view that there is no essential human nature and that man is free to create his own identity. His view, like the Catholic one, is that there is a permanent and universal essence to man. Free will for Burgess, as for all Catholics, is the choice of "whether or not to realize a given essential nature. Sartrean man invents his own essence."

The narrator of *A Clockwork Orange* is a fifteen-year-old named Alex who enjoys violence and whom the state selects for a brainwashing experiment aimed at making delinquents socially adjusted human beings. He tells his story in a teenage slang, Nadsat, a language invented by Burgess from Russian and from English cockney slang. The novel is set sometime in a future England and is the kind of science fiction which is fantasy only to the extent that it exaggerates certain tendencies found in the present world. Alex and his friends drink in milkbars that serve "milk plus something else"; drugs are widely used by the young. Juvenile crime, particularly of the violent kind, muggings, rapes, burglaries, has increased alarmingly; the old cry out for law and order. Everyone watches world TV.

It is a dreary world which appears to have been socialized, perhaps communised. The equation of socialism, which he claims in later novels springs from a mistaken view that man is perfectible, with a depressing sameness and loss of identify is typical of Burgess. The Russian influence apparent in the teenage slang Alex speaks has affected other aspects of life also. The municipal apartment building where Alex's family lives has a painting on the hallway wall of the dignity of labor; his mother shops in a statemart. God has been reduced to an "Old Bog"; the state is in control.

Burgess maintains a careful balance between the fantasy world he has created and our own. He begins the novel with Alex's long and detailed descriptions of his acts of violence, shocking the reader by the discrepancy between tone and subject: "at one place I ran over something big with a snarling toothy rot in the head-lamps, then it screamed and squelched under and Old Dim at the back near laughed his gulliver off — 'Ho ho ho' — at that." This, of course, seems at first like fantasy, partly because of the language. But Burgess keeps us constantly aware of the similarities between the horrors of the fantasy and those of our own world. His aim is not the alienation of the reader, but acceptance of this violence as an innate part of human nature.

The first vision we are given is of a free Alex. Alex runs a gang of boys who beat up an old man coming home from a library and enjoy killing the wife of an author whose house they gain admittance to, an incident based on Burgess's own life. After several initial descriptions of the violence, Burgess tells us about Alex's passion for classical music; when he is not out with his gang he spends his time listening to Beethoven, Mozart, Bach on his stereo equipment. The reader is slightly uneasy. Violent criminals are not supposed to enjoy classical music. What is worse, Alex fantasizes about his violent assaults to the Brandenburg Concerto. Either our responses to violence or our associations with classical music must be in question here. Alex describes an article he once read: "Great music, it said, and Great Poetry would like quieten Modern Youth down and make Modern Youth more civilized. Civilized my syphilised yarbles. Music always sort of sharpened me up, O my brothers."

The second vision Burgess gives us is of a conditioned Alex. Caught by the police, Alex is in prison, the object of an experiment called the Ludovico technique. This technique involves injecting Alex with a substance which will make him nauseated and then forcing him to watch films of violence. The theory is that he will associate sickness with violence and be unable to act violently again. It works. But Burgess, whose vision of the free Alex horrified us, makes it clear that he considers a conditioned Alex worse. He is now merely a thing.

At first, the reason for Burgess's disapproval of the conditioning seems clear enough. Alex has been deprived of the capacity for moral choice. In his interview with Churchill, Burgess said, "Choice, choice is all that matters, and to impose the good is evil, to *act* evil is better than to have good imposed." In the novel it is the chaplain who expresses this point of view: "He has no real choice, has he? He ceases to be a wrong-doer. He ceases also to be a creature capable of moral choice." But are we to believe this Chaplain who is a far from admirable character, smelling of liquor as he preaches about divine suffering? He is capable of rationalizing any scruple he may have about the Ludovico technique, saying to Alex, "And yet, in a sense, in choosing to be deprived of the ability to make an ethical choice, you have in a sense really chosen the good. So I shall like to think." Ironically, he has always treated Alex as a thing anyway, calling him 6655321, his prison number.

A further question is raised about the significance of moral choice to this novel, when Burgess makes it clear that not only has Alex never exercised his power of moral choice, but is not likely to do so after he is returned to his former state. The novel ends with Alex signing a piece of paper for the government, "not knowing what I was signing and not, O my brothers, caring either."

If it is wrong to condition someone like Alex out of his antisocial behavior, then it is wrong for a reason that goes beyond the question of moral choice. The clue lies perhaps in the passage from a book called *A Clockwork Orange* which Alex reads when he invades the author's home and kills his wife: "The attempt to impose upon man, a creature of growth and capable of sweetness, laws and conditions appropriate to a mechanical creation, against this I raise my sword-pen." Man may be capable of sweetness but as the following pages describing the gang's attack on the wife show us he is also capable of violence. The author of *A Clockwork Orange* in the novel is called F. Alexander; he is Burgess himself but also, as Alex realizes, "he is another Alex," a fact he amply demonstrates at the end of the novel in his desire for violent revenge on the person who killed his wife. The implication is, of course, that we are all violent by nature: Alex gets pleasure from reading the violent parts of the Bible; the police are as brutal as the criminals; the old men in the library want their revenge; and how about the filmmakers who photographed the violence Alex is forced to watch? "You couldn't imagine them being allowed to take these films without like interfering with what was going on."

What we think of as good and bad are both equally parts of human nature, a passion for violence and a passion for classical music. Human nature is composed of opposites, is a duality. As Alex explains: "More, badness is of the self . . . they of the government and the judges and the schools cannot allow the bad because they cannot allow the self." Man may find violence socially inconvenient but cannot claim it needs explanation: "They don't go into what is the cause of goodness, so why of the other shop?" When man is made a thing he is inevitably deprived of all aspects of his humanness, his love of classical music as well as his tendency towards violence. Dr. Brodsky, practitioner of the Ludovico technique, explains: "Delimitation is always difficult. The world is one, life is one. The sweetest and most heavenly of activities partake in some measure of violence — the act of love, for instance; music for instance."

Finally Alex is returned to his natural state and the reader is left knowing he will commit more acts of violence. Burgess has presented us with two unattractive visions, but has made us see that the choice is not between "goodness" and "badness" but between a dual reality composed of good and bad and the neutrality of "thingness." Given these alternatives, the choice of life, and hence of the violence, seems inevitable.

Burgess's fable is constructed on a series of doubles: there are two characters called Alex; two visits to the old men in the library; two visits to the house of the author; two views of Alex's friends, as criminals and as policemen. The clarity of the pattern forces us to make comparisons. But Burgess's aim is our involvement. His use of the title of his own novel as the title of the author's book, . . . is employed here to suggest that Burgess is F. Alexander, "another Alex," and therefore partakes equally of the violence. Throughout the novel Alex addresses his readers as "O my brothers," a phrase with obvious implications of complicity. Finally the teenage slang, Nadsat, that Burgess invented for the novel, serves to include us also. Initially strange, the words of the language are learned by the reader as he learns any language by being constantly exposed to them. He is, in fact, conditioned as Alex was; the effect of Nadsat on the reader functions as an ironic comment on the novel itself.

The Wanting Seed, written before but published after *A Clockwork Orange,* is a fantasy in exactly the same sense as the other novel. It posits a future England where overpopulation has reached mammoth proportions and drastic measures have been taken to combat the problem. Just as in *A Clockwork Orange,* the reader is initially shocked by being presented with a world in which all the accepted values are reversed. Heterosexuality is discouraged, homosexuality the norm; no one is allowed to have more than two children; the dead are used to fertilize the ground. Again the subject and the casual tone in which it is described are at variance: "Beatrice-Joanna Foxe snuffled a bereaved mother's grief as the little corpse, in its yellow plastic casket, was handed over to the two men from the ministry of Agriculture (Phosphorus Reclamation Department). They were cheerful creatures, coal-faced and with shining dentures, and one of them sang a song which had recently become popular."

Once more Burgess keeps the reader midway between his own world and the fantasy world of his creation, though the recent stress on the problems of population and the campaign to limit families to two children have brought the fantasy nearer our world than Burgess perhaps intended. In the novel overcrowding has made it necessary for children to go to school in shifts, some at night, and for London to spread as far as Brighton. The place names anchor the fantasy in an actual England, however, as does the description of cricket as the sacred game.

In the interview with Thomas Churchill, Burgess stated that *The Wanting Seed* is a Catholic book: "it's a very Catholic book. It's a total vindication of the encyclical. You know, of course, what the encyclical leaves out of account is the acceptance of natural checks, you know, is in fact Malthusianism. Malthus has always been condemned by the church, yet the church will now accept Malthusianism, at least tacitly. What's going to happen to our excess population? 'Well, Nature will take care of it,' as Malthus said, in other words, wars and pestilence, earthquakes."

If the novel functions as a defense of the encyclical on birth control, it is also a defense of Burgess's own view of reality as duality. In the book Burgess expresses his view as a defense of the Augustinian against the Pelagian doctrine, this time in terms of history rather than those of psychology. History is seen as a cycle of alternating and opposed attitudes, the Pelagian and the Augustinian. Tristram, hero of the novel, explains that the Pelagian view is liberal. The name is that of the monk Pelagius, who "denied the doctrine of Original Sin and said that man was capable of working out his own salvation." If man is perfectible then society by regulation and state control can be made perfect. Thus Pelagianism leads to socialism and communism. It is the disappointment at the failure of this society, Burgess claims, which leads to an interphase and then gradually back to Augustinianism.

The Augustinian is the opposed thesis, that man is inherently sinful and needs redemption through divine grace. This view, Tristram explains, leads to "conservatism and other laissez-faire and non-progressive political beliefs." When human nature turns out to be better than any pessimistic Augustinian could have expected, the interphase begins again and eventually Pelagianism is returned. Burgess stresses the cyclical and inevitable nature of history in *The Wanting Seed,* and in spite of his comment that he is concerned with choice and free will in this novel, none of the characters, except possibly Beatrice, exercises it, anymore than Alex does in *A Clockwork Orange.* Burgess gives the impression of a deterministic universe.

The first vision of *The Wanting Seed* is the end of a Pelagian phase. Man is in control, has turned God into a comic cartoon character for children to laugh at, Mr. Livedog. Man's efforts to control the problems of over-population, which have led to synthetic foods, the encouragement of homosexuality, the use of the dead as fertilizer, have been attempts to stabilize the society. Heterosexuality, the joining of the yin and the yang, a duality, is discouraged because it inevitably brings change, not stability. Beatrice and Tristram, husband and wife, are separated in this section of the novel. As a result of these denials of life, comes famine. Emma, Tristram's sister, writes that the rice crops have failed in Fukien Province in China; at Shonny's farm, where Beatrice goes to have her illegal twins, the hens won't lay and the pigs die. By the Fall the earth is afflicted with an unknown blight: "fruit fell off the trees and the hedges, stricken with a sort of gangrene. . . . And then there was the animal world: worms, coccidiosis, scaly leg, marble bone disease." Burgess uses the unpleasantness of such descriptions as this to emphasize that the Pelagian philosophy is wrong. It is that life-denying neutrality which is evil in Burgess's scheme.

The second vision of the novel is of a world becoming Augustinian once more. Everywhere Tristram travels he comes across heterosexual orgies. Life is returning; "all life was one. That blight had been man's refusal to breed." But with the return of life comes a return of the natural checks the Pelagian government had removed: war and cannibalism, the opposite of breeding. "It was reported . . . that a vast communal nocturnal gorge of man-flesh had been followed by a heterosexual orgy in the ruddy light of the fat-spitting fires and that, the morning after, the root known as salsify was seen sprouting from the pressed earth." The acceptance of life involves the acceptance of both the good and bad composing the duality of reality. The recognition that there is innate evil, an Augustinian attitude, brings back the necessity for God. "In Him we become one with all things, and He is one with all things and with us." Nevertheless, Burgess shows that the return to Pelagianism is inevitable in spite of the reconciliation of Beatrice and Tristram at the end of the novel.

The Wanting Seed, like *A Clockwork Orange,* is constructed on obvious doubles: the day versus the night, "Pelagian day, Augustinian
night"; twin brothers Derek and Tristram, the Pelagian and the Augustinian, later repeated in Beatrice's twins also called Derek and Tristram;
"The human dichotomy. The division. Contradictions. Instincts tell us
one thing and reason tells us another." The structure of the novel forces
us to compare the separate journeys of Beatrice and Tristram. At the
beginning alternate chapters are devoted to each, the link between them
being a word or phrase carried over from the final sentence of one chapter
to the first of the next. Chapter 4 ends: " 'What, sir,' asked Bellingham,
'is the cold-water treatment?' " Chapter 5 opens: "Beatrice-Joanna, the
waste of life-giving cold-water behind her, entered the open mouth of
the Ministry." Just as in *A Clockwork Orange,* Burgess has presented us
with two unattractive visions and through the relentless logic of the fable
method forced us to prefer his view of a dual reality over neutrality.

Tremor of Intent is not a fantasy novel in the same sense as *A
Clockwork Orange* and *The Wanting Seed.* It is not science fiction, but
takes place in a world very definitely that of the cold war period of postwar
Europe. It is a spy-thriller, of the kind practiced by Ian Fleming and E.
Howard Hunt, fantasy only to the extent that Burgess has deliberately exaggerated some of the characteristics of the form. As Geoffrey Aggeler
says, "The typical Bond feats of appetite are duplicated and surpassed,
sometimes to a well-nigh ridiculous extent." Indeed the gastronomic and
sexual excesses of someone like James Bond pale beside those of Burgess's
hero, Hillier. He becomes involved in a shipboard eating competition
with Mr. Theodorescu and in a scene of sexual acrobatics with Miss Devi,
Theodorescu's assistant, who has learned to give pleasure from Indian sex
manuals.

But Burgess explodes the spy-thriller form by relating its essential
characteristic, sensationalism, to the evil of the book, Mr. Theodorescu.
Hillier, who describes himself as subject to satyriasis and gluttony, a
duality he claims tends to cancel itself out, sacrifices both at the end of
the novel. The novel, with its surface story of spy intrigue, is actually the
account of Hillier's spiritual regeneration after a mock death; "He had
been discharged dead, after all. Only after death, he had once said, was
regeneration possible." Burgess has turned a superficial form into a metaphysical fable. There is, he appears to believe, some natural connection
between metaphysics and spying. Wriste, the steward on board, says
"Perhaps all of us who are engaged in this sort of work — international intrigue, espionage, scarlet pimpernellianism, hired assassination — seek

something deeper than what most people term life, meaning a pattern of simple gratifications."

Tremor of Intent recounts Hillier's last spy mission before his retirement, a mission which involves a journey to Russia to return to England a scientist who has defected. The scientist, Roper, is an old school fellow of Hillier's. The choice Burgess is offering us is apparently once again a choice between the Pelagian and Augustinian views of the universe. When we first see Roper at school, he attacks his Catholic teachers with rational arguments and believes that the world is ultimately knowable through science. Hillier writes to his superiors about Roper: "If he's a heretic at all it's your heresy he subscribes to — the belief that life can be better and man nobler. It's not up to me, of course, to say what a load of bloody nonsense that is." Hillier associates this Pelagian view of human perfectibility with state control, with a tendency towards loss of full humanity: Roper "was turning into a thing, growing out of boyhood into thinghood, not manhood." We expect the usual Burgess condemnation of this attitude, particularly since Hillier is associated with St. Augustine and shares with Burgess an Augustinian pessimism and a belief in the fundamental sinfulness of human beings.

On board ship, however, Burgess's second vision of Hillier reveals that Hillier's true enemy is not communism or Pelagianism but those qualities represented by Mr. Theodorescu. Mr. Theodorescu is a neutral "in the pay of no power, major or minor." He is homosexual, and homosexuality here, as elsewhere in Burgess's novels, is used to suggest a denial of life, a denial of the great duality. Like Hillier, Theodorescu has used gluttony and self-indulgence as a way of avoiding real commitment. For Hillier, who describes himself as "nothing more than a superior technician," is, he discovers, a neutral too. Alan, a boy he meets on the ship, finally accuses him: "Bloody neutrals. That bitch with the grief-stricken headache and filthy Theodorescu and grinning Wriste and *you*."

This neutrality, as in *A Clockwork Orange* and *The Wanting Seed*, is the real evil. The choice is between a reality which includes both capitalism and communism, Catholicism and Protestantism, Pelagianism and Augustinianism, and neutrality. Roper, foolishly running from one faith to another, is at least committed and therefore preferable to the Theodorescus. Finally able to inform an intention of his own, Hillier kills Theodorescu and becomes a priest in order to fight in the war between God and Not god, "The two sides of the coin of ultimate reality," "the war of which temporal wars are just a mere copy."

The concept of the game is important to this novel and Hillier's progress is marked by a change in his attitude to the significance of the war he is fighting. Early in the novel, he tells Theodorescu that spying is a game, "a great childish game on the floor of the world"; he explains that we play it because we don't believe in good and evil anymore. "If we don't play it, what else are we going to play? We're too insignificant to be attacked by either the forces of light or the forces of darkness." Alan tells him that games are all right for children but not for adults, and aligns Hillier's game-playing with the idea of neutrality. Hillier's final realization is that "The big war can be planned here as well as anywhere"; the game on the floor of the world is a copy of the big war and as such must be taken seriously.

As in *A Clockwork Orange,* Burgess sets up a false choice and then reveals the true one. The pattern is again made obvious through the striking use of doubles: death must be compensated for by the other half of the duality, procreation. When Hillier's father dies, he is afflicted with spermatorrhea, and is told it is "an unconscious assertion of the progenitive impulse." Miss Devi, the dark assistant of Mr. Theodorescu, is balanced by Clara, a fair-haired sixteen-year-old. The structure of the novel is a series of double scenes: the first visit to Miss Devi is balanced by the second; the sexual experience of Miss Devi is balanced by that with Clara; Hillier's letter with Roper's confession; the great eating scene with the scene of Hillier's destruction of Theodorescu in which he literally stuffs the villain with information. Burgess forces upon us the necessary degree of detachment so that we can perceive the metaphysical fable underneath the spy-thriller. Form echoes theme brilliantly for the spy-thriller form here is an imposture, a game version of a metaphysical fable, just as the war between good and evil on earth imitates that in heaven.

Part of *Enderby* was originally published as *Inside Mr. Enderby* under the pseudonym Joseph Kell. The novel *Enderby* as it now stands in the edition published in the United States presents two visions of a poet. In the first and last parts, posterity, through a fantasy visit of a schoolmaster and a group of unappreciative school children, is watching the sleeping Enderby. Only in this way does the reader learn that Enderby has become a major poet, whose poems are assigned as set books for national examinations. Ironically, in becoming important Enderby has become an object; the children have to be reminded that he is "not a thing to be prodded; he is a great poet sleeping." "Thingness" is what Enderby, whose life is seen from his own point of view in the rest of the novel, has been avoiding all his life. While living he is a minor poet, not included in the anthologies, hardly known, with only the slightest intimation of the fantasy visit of posterity which he apprehends as a dream.

The part of the novel concerning Enderby's life seen from his point of view is fantasy only in the sense that the action is exaggerated, possible but improbable. Nevertheless, in spite of the fact that the exaggeration serves primarily to make this a very comic book, similar in many ways to Joyce Cary's *The Horse's Mouth,* and the fact that the skeleton of Burgess's fable is much more fleshed than in the earlier novels, the same basic theme is here. Art depends on a choice of the duality of life over the neutrality of non-life.

In the first part of the novel Enderby is living in a furnished apartment in a seaside town in England in total disorder, eating badly, mostly on scraps given him by the local bartender, sleeping in his clothes, rarely bathing, using the bathtub to hold notes, books, ink bottles, cigarette-packets, and scraps of leftover food. Masturbation has taken the place of sexual activity with women, and he is obsessed by his late stepmother, whose loathsome personal habits he hated as a child.

The ambiguity of Enderby's relationship to his stepmother, whose life-style he has in part imitated, whose strong tea is always a comfort to him, continues throughout the book. In one sense she is the ugliness and vitality of the reality he needs in order to write, his sexual feelings for her the guilt which is "creation's true dynamo." In another she is the false mother. About to have sexual relations with Vesta, he thinks "that it was a mother he had always wanted, not a stepmother, and he had made that mother himself in his bedroom, made her out of the past, history, myth, the craft of verse. When she was made, she became slimmer, younger, more like a mistress; she became the Muse." Every real woman is a stepmother to Enderby, and he is prevented by the Muse, his true mother, from having sexual relations with her. Enderby is, therefore, impotent; true sexual consummation for him is the creation of a poem. Burgess echoes the Joycean statement in *Portrait of the Artist* of the essential identity of the aesthetic, sexual, and spiritual impulses.

The dual nature of Enderby's life in this first part of the novel, composed of dirt and beauty, is summed up in the image of the lavatory, Enderby's "poetic seat." His poetry is written here, partly to suggest the function of art as time's cleanser and cathartiser, partly to suggest "a cell, smallest unit of life" which is all that is necessary for art. Most of all, though, it conveys that duality which to Burgess is the essential nature of reality. The reader's association with excrement and poetry are obviously in opposition to one another.

In the second part of the novel, Vesta Bainbridge, who works for a woman's magazine called *Fem* attempts to separate the poet in Enderby from the disorder of his antisocial life. She marries him and turns him into a clean, neat, well-ordered man, younger looking and better socialized. But this life is a non-life, artificial like its creator; like Vesta, whose upper-class accent becomes working class when she is excited, it is a mere veneer. When Enderby leaves Vesta, he has realized the necessary connection between the disorder of his old life and the creative impulse: "And as for poetry; that's a job for anarchs. Poetry's made by rebels and exiles and outsiders, it's made by people on their own, not by sheep baaing bravo to the Pope. Poets don't need religion and they don't need bloody little cocktail-party gossip either; it's they who make language and make myths. Poets don't need anybody except themselves." Order, in other words, is something poets make through intercourse with reality; prepackaged order, like women, like religion, is a stepmother and merely in the way.

Once he returns to England from Rome, where he leaves Vesta during the honeymoon, Enderby finds his poetic gift has deserted him. He no longer feels the guilt, which, as he illustrates in his long narrative poem "The Pet Beast," is necessary for civilization. "The Pet Beast," as he explains to fellow-poet Rawcliffe, is the story of the story of the Minotaur, original sin, destroyed by "The Pelagian liberator, the man who had never known sin, the guilt-killer." Without original sin, in a Protestant world where there is "nothing sure and nothing mysterious," there is no art. Enderby attempts suicide and the state takes over his life, in the form of a state psychiatrist who makes him take his mother's name, Hogg— makes him become his mother not seduce her—and forget poetry. He becomes a bartender, the seller of wine not a consumer, once again in the wrong relationship for a poet to the life juices. Enderby/Hogg is prepared to join the Church of England. He is an ex-poet, an unfrocked priest, and as a neuter thing is evil, just as a conditioned Alex was in *A Clockwork Orange*. Rawcliffe, talking of his own loss of inspiration, explains: "The unfrocked priest does not become a mere neuter harmless being; he becomes evil. He has to be used by something, for super-nature abhors a supervacuum, so he becomes evil."

The linking of spiritual and artistic experience apparent in Rawcliffe's comments occurs again in the figures of Yod Crewsy and his Fixers, a group of pop-singers, who represent for Burgess degenerate religion and degenerate art. It is Hogg's resentment of Yod's plagiarizing of Enderby's poems that causes his violent attack upon Yod and subsequent regeneration as Enderby. Like Vesta from whom he obtains Enderby's poems, Yod Crewsy is mere veneer, a copy. He has a double in the novel in Rawcliffe, the homosexual poet, who has one poem in all the anthologies and who has also plagiarized from Enderby, taking his idea for "The Pet Beast" and turning it into a bad film. Enderby says of Crewsy to Rawcliffe: "He deserved to be shot. Plagiarism. A travesty of art. He stole my poems. The same as you."

Although the end of the novel doubles the begining — Rawcliffe in his dirt and excrement dying of cancer can finally write again briefly — there is less emphasis in *Enderby* on the duality of reality, which this doubling has dramatized in other Burgess novels. It is implied, however, in Enderby's need for disorder to create order. Although *Enderby* offers the usual Burgess choice between life and non-life of the earlier novels, three important themes here — incest, the mysteriousness of reality, and the nature of bad art — point towards his next novel, *MF*.

At the time of the Churchill interview, Burgess was working on *MF*. He described the novel in this way: "I want to write a structuralist novel. The first of the structuralist novels, I hope, based on the Lévi-Strauss theatre of the correlation between language and social forms. So that I want to exploit the Algonquin legend, the boy who was bound to commit incest because he could answer all the riddles correctly, which is a direct tie-up with Oedipus." Burgess's myth is the story of Miles Faber whose search for the works of a little-known poet, Sib Legeru, leads him to answering riddles set by monsters and birds, and ultimately to incest. As the double connotation of his initials suggests, the two implications are interwoven from the beginning. The initials stand for Miles Faber, Latin for "a soldier in the service of the craftsman," which is perhaps a ways of describing a riddle-solver, and also, of course, they stand for mother-fucker.

MF is an incredibly difficult book; Burgess has more than fulfilled the prophecy he made to Jim Hicks in 1968: "The sort of things I write will be more and more involuted, more and more difficult, less and less saleable. This just has to be. You get fed up with existing technique. You have to do something more daring." Burgess has dared to put the reader in the position of solving a whole series of riddles, not just those which Miles has to solve, but the riddles of the book itself. The reader is obviously intended to be placed in a position parallel to that of Miles, just as in *A Clockwork Orange* Nadsat conditioned the reader much as Alex was conditioned. *MF* is full of scraps of foreign languages — Sanskrit, Welsh, Italian, Indonesian — of conundrums, some of which Burgess has invented and some of which belong in folklore, of palinlogues, of every possible kind of word game.

To understand what Burgess is attempting here it is helpful to refer to two comments in his book on Joyce, who, after all, practiced many of these games before he did. The first concerns the significance of riddles and talks of the relationship between the mysteries of the cosmos and those of language. To Burgess, as to Joyce, there is more than a metaphorical connection between them: "The difficulties of *Ulysses* and, very much more, of *Finnegans Wake* are not so many tricks and puzzles and deliberate obscurities to be hacked at like jungle lianas: they represent those elements which surround the immediate simplicities of human society; they stand for history, myth, and the cosmos. Thus we have not merely to accept them but to regard them as integral."

The second is a comment about himself and the relationship between languages:

> Waking literature (that is literature that bows to time and space) is the exploitation of a single language. Dream-literature, breaking down all boundaries, may be more concerned with the phenomenon of language in general. Living in the West, I have little occasion to use Malay, a tongue I know at least as well as I know French. In dreams, I am no longer in the West; with the collapse of space, compass-points have no meaning. Hence English and Malay frequently dance together, merging, becoming not two languages conjoined but an emblem of language in general."

In *MF* Burgess uses many languages as an indication of a fundamental structure basic to all languages. The fact that the reader does not need a translation is itself an illustration of Burgess's point.

The relationship between apparently dissimilar languages, like the relationship between linguistic and social structures, is explained by Burgess in terms of the Lévi-Strauss theory that the mind of man has been operating in the same pattern since the beginning of time. This theory is obviously in opposition to the Sartrean denial of inherent structure in man or the universe and can very easily include the possibility of, though does not necessarily imply, what Burgess calls in *The Wanting Seed*, "a pattern-making demiurge." Merleau-Ponty points out in his article "From Mauss to Claude Lévi-Strauss": "Society itself is a structure of structures: how could there be absolutely no relationship between the linguistic system, the economic system, and the kinship system it employs?"

In the novel Burgess indicates the link between language and social forms by the similarity of the pronunciation of Keteki, name of the professor whose riddle Miles solves and who sends him on his journey, and Kitty Kee, nickname of Mile's sister whom he is forced to marry. Hence a parallelism is established between solving riddles and sleeping with one's sister. Throughout the novel Burgess draws the two concepts, "postures and language," together. Pardaleos explains: "We condemn incest because it's the negation of social communion. It's like writing a book in which every sentence is a tautology." Man's drive to reproduce himself is described as one of the "great structural machines throbbing away, those messages in code." As Burgess explains at the end of the novel: "Communication has been the whatness of the communication."

That the structure of two myths can be the same in two very separate cultures is in itself a confirmation of the structuralist theory. The significance of the myth used by Burgess here, a combination of the Algonquin legend and the Oedipus myth, is described by Lévi-Strauss in *Structural Anthropology:*

> The myth has to do with the inability, for a culture which holds the belief that mankind is autochthonous, to find a satisfactory transition between this theory and the knowledge that human beings are actually born from the union of man and woman. Although the problem obviously cannot be solved, the Oedipus myth provides a kind of logical tool which relates the original problem — born from one or born from two? — to the derivative problem: born from different or born from same? By a correlation of this type, the overrating of blood relations is to the underrating of blood relations as the attempt to escape autochthony is to the impossibility to succeed in it. Although experience contradicts theory, social life validates cosmology by its similarity of structure. Hence cosmology is true.

The myth cannot determine whether man is free, sprung from the earth itself, or whether he is bound by the structures that parental inheritance imply. Myths do not solve a problem, but by creating a balance between the opposing forces of the dilemma, they do provide a way of dealing with it.

Although Burgess's own comments on *MF* are a convenient way into any discussion of the novel, they are not necessary in order to understand his purpose. Clues lead back to the myths throughout the novel, but are particularly numerous in the first few chapters. Three epigraphs begin the novel. The first, "In his *Linguistic Atlas of the United States and Canada* Hans Karath recognizes no isogloss coincident with the political border along Latitude 49°N. — Simon Potter," links the ideas of language and culture together, and, as we learn some pages into the novel, is also a comment on the fact that the Iroquois and Algonquin tribes recognized no such border. It is also a reference to a central theme of the novel, that there is an evil in divisions; all life is one. The second is a French quotation about the impossibility of God's ever being understood without the French, which is probably a reference to Lévi-Strauss: "C'est embêtant, dit Dieu. Quand il n'y aura plus ces Français / Il y a des choses que je fais, il n'y aura plus personne pour les comprendre. — Charles Péguy." The third is a stage direction from *Much Ado about Nothing:* "Enter Prince, Leonato, Claudio, and Jacke Wilson — *Much Ado about Nothing,* First Folio," which is reference to Burgess's real name, John Anthony Burgess Wilson, and presumably a comic reference to this novel.

There are many references to the Algonquin myth. When the novel opens Miles is staying at the Algonquin Hotel; on TV he hears an Indian talking about the Weskerini and Nipissing tribes which he remembers "are members of the great Algonquin family"; he dreams of a toothless squaw surrounded by owls; he drinks a new soft drink called a Coco-Coho, meaning owl, in an owl-shaped bottle; Kitty, his sister, keeps her money in a little china owl; the name of Aderyn, who has a bird act in the circus, means owl in Welsh; her birds, who ask riddles, are named after contemporary novelists: Iris, Angus, Charles, Pamela, John, Penelope, Brigid, Anthony, Muriel, Mary, Norman, Saul, Philip, Ivy, presumably all askers of riddles.

There are an equally large number of references to the Oedipus myth: Loewe talks of a cocktail called a Clubfoot; Mr. Pardaleos refers to cultural taboos on incest, "Oedipus, Electra, all that," "This house of Atreus nonsense"; Llew tells Miles about the time Aderyn had a man from the audience answering the birds' questions "and if he got the answer wrong they'd all fly on to him like to peck his fucking jellies out"; Miles smokes Dji Sam Soe cigarettes which actually exist in Indonesia and have "2, 3, 4" on their package, a translation of Dji Sam Soe; Aspinwall drinks Azzopardis' White Cane Rum, a reference to both lameness and blindness; and if the reader has missed all this, Burgess has Miles at the end of the novel refer to Swellfoot the Tyrant, "a man with a clubfoot" who "had once answered the unanswerable and moved on to sleep with his mother." To suggest to the reader that the connection between the myths confirms structural anthropological theory, there are various references to people called Strauss, to Richard and Johann through titles of their compositions, and later to "Strauss and the Romantic School."

Burgess trains the reader to solve the riddles by demonstrating how. "Up, I am a rolling river; Down a scent-and-color-giver" gives flower, we are told. As the novel progresses Burgess expects the reader to solve them himself, but invariably gives the answer obliquely in the following sentence. For example, three riddles, the answer to which are Breath, Mouth, and Heart, are followed by the sentence, "The breath grew sour in my mouth, and my heart pumped hard." This is one of Burgess's methods of keeping the reader parallel to Miles, in the same relation to the experience of the novel.

In a conversation with the monstrous Gonzi halfway through the novel, Miles learns the purpose of myths: "Only by entry into myth can reconciliation be effected." *MF* is the story of Miles's entry into myth and of his reconciliation with the structural pattern of the great duality. In order to suggest the idea of resurrection this implies, Burgess employs yet another myth, the Christian one. Miles was born on Christmas Eve; his twin's name is Llew or Noel. The miracle of Senta Euphorbia, which involves the emission of blood from the penis of the statue of Jesus, is foreshadowed when Miles earlier suffers the same problem on board the plane. The dead body of Llew mysteriously disappears from its hiding place. The final section of the novel contains an image of the hanged man, which relates Christ to Oedipus, "That poor Greek kid hanging from a tree by a twig thrust through his foot."

Miles's entry into reality is defined primarily, however, in terms of freedom versus structure. The first vision of the novel is of Miles in New York. He has just taken part in a protest demonstration which included having sexual intercourse in the open air with a fellow student called Carlotta Tukang. He views this as a gesture of freedom and in a conversation with his lawyer, Loewe, the first of many lions in the novel, expresses in Existentialist terms his belief in his own freedom. "I'm a free man," he says to Loewe; later to himself, "I could, like the imagined work of Sib Legeru, be wholly free."

He wants "the death of form and the shipwreck of order" and expects to find it in the work of Sib Legeru, poet of free verse. The works of Sib Legeru are supposedly in Castita where they have been placed by Sir James Pismire. Miles is also trying to avoid a marriage with a Miss Ang, arranged by his father whose own incestuous background has led him to believe in creative miscegenation. What to his father is a way of avoiding incestuous bondage is a restriction to Miles. The careful reader is suspicious of Miles's search for reality and meaning in Sib Legeru (Sibyl Guru), from the beginning. The name Pismire and the name of Miles's substitute mother, Miss Emmett, are names of ants, those models of social organization, who, in a Burgess novel, must be trusted.

Nevertheless, at the beginning of the novel, Miles believes he can create his own world; at this point he invents the riddles, creating word puzzles on the names of Loewe and Pardaleos. He does not appear to notice the synthetic nature of the world where man is in control, where the soup is instant, where no one enjoys violence, gets "no kicks from mugging," where emotions are "not to be engaged," and we must "school ourselves to new modes of feeling, unfeeling rather." Here the sexual impulse is perverted, as in the scene with the impotent Chester and his girl Irma. This world is an Electronic Village where the link between people is artificial; it is the lifeless neutral one which Burgess wished us to reject in *A Clockwork Orange, The Wanting Seed,* and *Tremor of Intent.*

The second vision of *MF* is the world of Grencjita (Green City) in Castita (Chastity), the world of doubles, paradoxes, and riddles where Miles learns the truth. It is undoubtedly significant that there are so many references to Shakespeare in the novel, for this second world functions much as the world of Shakespeare's romances, as a place where all is put right. Miles travels to this country on a "Pluribus" run by "Unum" airlines, *ex pluribus unum* being a way of expressing Burgess's view of reality, and on a boat belonging to two homosexuals, Pine Chandeleur and Aspinwall. They seem to be examples of the two worlds, New York and Castita; as homosexuals in a Burgess novel they belong to the neutral world, yet they also represent the world of paradox. Burgess makes a point of stressing how different the two men are, says they "were free, though in desperate sexual bondage to each other," and has Pine Chandeleur wear a shirt upon which are printed such religious paradoxes as "The more God is in all things, the more He is outside them."

Castita is more obviously a fantasy world. Here a religious procession turns into a circus, monsters ask riddles, men meet their doubles. Hints, clues, and the fact of the fantasy itself keep the reader in position of riddle solver. The most important doubles in Castita are the two men, Z. Fonanta and Mr. Gonzi, who ask Miles riddles at the end of an open-air meeting soon after his arrival in the city. The answers to the riddles they ask are the male and female sex organs, the yin/yang of reality, and these two men are representatives of the opposing halves of the duality. Zoon Fonanta, we learn, means the talking animal, man. In the novel he is

Miles's grandfather, the boss who is in control of everything: "Dr. Fonanta sets the pattern like." The pattern of the mind of man, in Lévi-Strauss terms, is universal and is the origin of all. Mr. Gonzi, Italian for *fool*, is the representative of darkness, Mr. Dunkel in the novel. Leonine and deformed, he is obviously intended to take the place of the sphinx in the myth. The riddle which Miles is finally forced to answer is his own name, "Gonzi," perhaps suggesting the complete self-absorption, that inward turning incest partly represents.

The other important set of doubles Miles meets are his own brother and sister, Llew and Kitty. Miss Emmett calls Llew "The bad Miles." Like Alex in *A Clockwork Orange*, Miles has both good and bad within him. Llew, another Lion, is identical to Miles in appearance, different only in voice and background. Miles dislikes the similarity because of Llew's violence and vulgarity and welcomes the minor differences: "To me his voice . . . was the hateful blessed key to a return to the total variousness of life against which he and I were blaspheming." Ironically, Llew shares Mile's philosophy of life, is son of Aderyn, the bird woman in the circus, and does an escape act for which he is billed "Llew the Free." Miles and Llew become interchangeable after Miles has murdered Llew for attempting to rape his sister and thus is forced to sleep with his sister himself. According to the myth the underrating of blood relations, the murder of kin, is balanced by the overrating of blood relations, incest: " 'You,' Aderyn said 'are Miles Faber. That girl is your sister. You have committed the worst deadly sin, and it must be only to cover up the twin of that sin which is murder.' "

Meanwhile Miles has discovered the works of Sib Legeru, coincidentally concealed by Sir James Pismire in the house where his sister is staying. Coincidence in *MF* is indicative of a patterned universe, not of a universe ruled by chance. The poems of Sib Legeru appear to Miles to illustrate complete freedom, as he had expected them to. But, as Fonanta explains later to Miles, they are in fact structured "on the meanest and most irrelevant of taxonomies, they derive their structure from the alphabetic arrangements of encyclopedias and dictionaries." They are also creations of Fonanta. The very same Sib Legeru means in Anglo-Saxon to sleep with one's kin or incest, so Miles in search of freedom had been also in search of incest. Incest as taboo breaking is a false freedom, just as the works of Sib Legeru are pseudo-literary works. "It is a man's job to impose manifest order on the universe, not to yearn for Chapter Zero of the Book of Genesis."

Miles learns also that Tukang means craftsman, as does Faber, so that his initial act of protest with Carlotta Tukang was in a sense incestuous too. "The whole of the stupid past is our father," and so in a sense exogamy is incest. Miles finally recognizes that "nobody's free." He accepts marriage with Miss Ang, who is presumably the Ethel of the final chapter of the novel, and the reader learns, to his surprise, that Miles is black. Their marriage, then, is an example of "creative miscegenation."

The statement of the book is a statement about the duality and mystery of the structure of the universe. The nature of a paradox is its unanswerability: "For order has both to be and not to be challenged, this being the anomalous condition of the sustention of the cosmos. Rebel becomes hero; witch becomes saint. Exogamy means disruption and also stability; incest means stability and also disruption. You've got to have it both ways." The universe is not irrational but ordered; man in search of total liberty will only find prison.

Burgess says, "the story I've told is more true than plausible," and he reverses the self-conscious art technique to ask us to believe in the fantasy. "Believe that I said what follows," says Miles at the beginning, later adding, "I recognize the difficulty my reader is now going to experience in accepting what I wish to be accepted as a phenomenon of real life and not as a mere property of fiction." Burgess, like Joyce, has used his novel to show that the disparate parts of human experience are one. All is "a seamless unity." There are no borders among language, behavior, geography, anatomy. There are also hints that *MF*, like Joyce's *Portrait*, follows other structural schemes. There is a suspiciously large number of trees referred to. There is a suggestion of the life cycle: we start with figs (the big-bosomed lady, F. Carica) and progress to milk producers (Euphorbia). And what of all the lions? The parts of the body? Some riddles, as Burgess warns, must be left unanswered.

Like all novelists of nightmare, Burgess takes us towards the mystery of infinity not the nothingness of the void. He answers the post-Existential premise that the world is irrational by a leap of faith that what we see is mystery not muddle. Each novel is constructed on a pattern of doubles to suggest a patterned, and therefore meaningful universe. His technique forces the reader to reconstruct the pattern, to fit the pieces together in an all-inclusive picture. The act of reading a novel of nightmare, like the act of writing it is, then, itself a way of transcending the post-Existential dilemma.

ESTHER PETIX

Linguistics, Mechanics, and Metaphysics: A Clockwork Orange

The second half of the twentieth century has passively acknowledged the emergence of its most controversial gadfly, John Anthony Burgess Wilson: philosopher, critic, theologian, linguist, musician, academician, and author. Yet the seemingly facile task of the Burgess critic is not so much a matter of ascribing priorities within Burgess's various spheres of expertise, but rather (and amazingly) in shouldering the onus of redressing the dearth of any critical attention. Serious and exhaustive research reveals that Burgess's tremendous energy and soaring imagination have netted only moderate acclaim, a modicum of intellectual authority, and a quasi-reputation as one of the century's comic artists. For too long Burgess's literary precision and satire have been obscured beneath labels of precocious, light wit. While his contemporaries moved to the heights of fame and fortune, garnering critical attention, esteem, and aggrandizement, the wealth of Burgess's knowledge and ingenuity within the form of the novel remained ignored.

Most certainly Burgess has his following, but his disciples' enthusiasm (at times almost hysteria) has not diverted attention to his themes, nor has it acquainted large numbers with the universality of his traditionalism and messages. Perhaps, then, he is in need of one fewer disciple and one more evangelist. For as any devotee of Burgess knows, this is an era that enjoys the dramatic sweep of technocracy. Today one

From *Old Lines, New Forces: Essays on the Contemporary British Novel, 1960-1970,* edited by Robert K. Morris. © 1976 by Associated University Presses. Fairleigh Dickinson University Press, 1976.

must introduce status (of any sort) from the point of volume rather than quality or essence, and by contemporary standards, shibboleths, and axioms, Burgess's work is not established. In terms of sheer physical output, Burgess ranks high. Compared with the popularity of contemporaries, however, Burgess's sales offer only tepid comparison.

That Burgess is not a top seller has many implications. First, and obviously, there are distinct implications for Burgess himself. As a professional author, he is certainly aware of market returns to his own purse; aware, too, that what and how much he sells has a material effect upon his own life-style, if not his *raison d'être*. Unyieldingly, however, he tends toward remoteness and obscurity, holding out in effect for principle over capital. Ideally, Burgess's stand is consistent with his philosophy.

The implications for the reading public are another matter. Why, for example, is Burgess considered intellectually obscure? Why, after nearly thirty books, must one still introduce him as "the author of *A Clockwork Orange*," and that reference only recognizable because of the barely recognizable film version (call it rather, perversion) of the novel? An obvious problem exists when an author who has so much to say and is possessed of such profundities is not widely read; is, in fact, dismissed as a perpetrator of violence or as a comic. But then, Burgess criticism is at best confused. It is further obfuscated by the fact that he holds sway over a devoted following (which includes some first-rate critics), yet does not hold commensurate stature among scholars. It is my contention that the major force of Burgess has been siphoned off into static frenetics rather than into direct qualitative evaluation. That a clouding of Burgess's fiction has occurred is patent; how and why it has occurred requires a deeper analysis of Burgess's fiction and mind, both of which are labyrinthine. The labyrinth, a symbol often invoked by Burgess himself, is charted with the aid of various threads and clues running through his fiction. And pursuing these leads, these seeming difficulties, these ambiguities, these strata and substrata brings the reader to the inner core of Burgess's central satire: the Minotaur's Cave.

As a maze-maker, Burgess challenges not only Dedalus in the manner of construction, but God in the act of creation — a device and theory he learned from Joyce. Yet such creations and constructs demand a more formal system, and often an elusive one. Like the protagonist, the reader is drawn through threads of the literal plot into the maze, formed often as not below the author's own hilarious crust of ego. Yet, concurrently, Burgess as readily hides himself in the center of his creation, sequestered and insulated by its vastness as well as its intricacies. Readers thus are invited, nay dared, to master the maze, to pick up the various threads and wander the labyrinth; but the same reader always comes to the mystical center—volitionally, and only after much effort.

Imperfectly read, Burgess is necessarily open to charges of philosophical bantering; misread he is often missed entirely. It remains, then, to follow those distinct, definitive threads designed by the architect himself which lead to the mind of the maze-builder, the "God-rival." For at the center the reader may discover an entire universe in which the author attempts to contain the human colony. As with all artists who attempt to match wits with God, Burgess provides only a scale model. Yet it is a model unique in many vital, identifiable ways. Stated as a more classical apostrophe, Burgess constructs his cosmogony to explain—there is no longer in the modern world any need to justify or vindicate—the ways of man to man: to see hope through failure; to set a course while adrift; to seek certainty in ambiguity. In following the threads leading into the center of the labyrinth, we are able to spin from Burgess's fictions something of our own identities.

Midway in Burgess's decade of authorship, and bleakest within his fictional cosmogony, are the years of the early sixties. It is a period marked by excessive concern with death (his own seeming imminent) and with protagonists only thinly disguised as alter-egos. Added to a medical diagnosis of (suspected) brain tumor were England's failures through socialism, her displacement as a world power in the aftermath of World War II, and her lack of character among the modern nations. All this greeted Burgess upon his return home from the Far East. In facing his own death, he also faced the demise of England. And the twofold bitterness is reflected in a twin-bladed satire so lacerating and abrasive that it goes beyond satire into black comedy.

In 1962 Burgess published his two dystopian novels, *The Wanting Seed* and *A Clockwork Orange*. Both are horrible visions of the future, predicated upon the present. In essence what Burgess does in the two novels is to project socialism and the excesses of the Welfare State (*A Clockwork Orange*) and historical behaviorism (*The Wanting Seed*) into a future that is at once nebulous and contemporary. Through such an extension in time he contends that socialism leads to a loss of the will and behaviorism leads to a loss of the soul. These companion novels consider the impact of original sin, abortion, cannibalism, violence, and free will on human beings who daily grow more will-less and more soulless.

However bleak the authorial outlook, however black the comedy, Burgess in his dystopian mood is Burgess at his most lucid. No longer are the protagonists culled from Establishment posts: Ennis of *A Vision of Battlements* was a soldier; Crabbe of "the Malayan Trilogy" was a civil servant; Howarth, of *The Worm and the Ring,* was a schoolteacher. Now the anti-hero of Burgess has become a full-blown rebel, and the quiescent, or slightly recalcitrant Minotaur is savage and obvious. One must keep this in mind in turning to *A Clockwork Orange,* for it is not only Burgess's best-known novel; it is Burgess at his most exposed, and perhaps most vulnerable.

The central thematic and structural interrogative of the novel comes when the prison "charlie" (chaplain) laments: "Does God want goodness or the choice of goodness? Is a man who chooses the bad perhaps in some way better than a man who has the good imposed upon him?" Such a question, while it affords the concision necessary to a reviewer, is totally insufficient to the critic. For there is something at once delightful and horrible, dogged and elusive in *A Clockwork Orange* that even so profound a rhetorical question cannot contain. There is something about the novel so frightening that it demanded a new language, and something so immanent in the message of the novel that it refused to be separated from the language. Linguistics and metaphysics — the how and what of *A Clockwork Orange* — are the disparate, yet connected threads leading to the Minotaur.

A Clockwork Orange is in part a clockwork, not merely titularly, but essentially. Its cadence and regularity are a masterpiece of grotesque precision. The reader is as much a flailing victim of the author as he is a victim of time's finite presence. He is hurtled into a futuristic book of twenty-one chapters and comes to acknowledge that he, as well as the protagonist-narrator, Alex, is coming of age; that he, too, is charged with advancement and growth. This "initiation" aspect of the novel is not gratuitous — of course. For the novel is further divided into three parts, reminiscent of the three ages of man; and each of these three parts begins with the question scanning the infinite and the indefinite: "What's it going to be then, eh?" Added to both of these devices is the haunting and vaguely familiar setting of the novel that teases the reader into an absurdly disquieting sense of regularity — as numbers have a way of doing — all the more unnerving because such regularity conveys a sense of rhythm about to be destroyed.

The novel's tempo, and its overwhelming linguistic accomplishment is to a great degree based upon the language Nadsat, coined for the book: the language of the droogs and of the night. It is the jargon of rape, plunder, and murder veiled in unfamiliarity, and as such it works highly successfully. Anthony De Vitis asserts that Nadsat may be an anagram for Satan'd, but Burgess insists on the literal Russian translation of the word for "teen." The novel makes a fleeting reference to the origins of the language. "Odd bits of old rhyming slang . . . a bit of gipsy talk, too. But most of the roots are Slav. Propaganda. Subliminal penetration."

Close examination of the language reveals a variety of neologisms applied in countless ways. First, there is the overwhelming impact of a Russianate vocabulary that is concurrently soothing and unnerving to the reader. It most certainly softens the atrocities of the book. It is far simpler, for example, to read about a "krovvy-covered plot" or "tolchock-ing an old veck" than it is to settle into two hundred pages of "blood-covered bodies" or "beatings of old men." The author keeps his audience absorbed in the prolonged violence through the screen of another language. But the Russian has a cruelty of its own; and there are dis-quieting political undercurrents in Burgess's imposition of Slavic upon English, at least for the tutored ear.

Nadsat, like all of Burgess's conventional writing, harbors a number of skillful puns. People are referred to as "lewdies"; the "charlie/charles" is a chaplain; "cancers" are cigarettes; and the "sinny" is the cinema. There is, to be sure, little room for laughter in a novel as sobering as this, and Burgess's usual authorial grin is only suggested in this very bitter glimpse of tomorrow. Still, there is no absence of satire. In many ways Alex is still a youth, and the reader is repeatedly shocked by a profusion of infantilisms starkly juxtaposed with violence. Burgess flecks his dialogue of evil with endearing traces of childhood in words like "appy polly loggies," "skolliwoll," "purplewurple," "baddiwad," or "eggiwegg" for "apologies," "school," "purple," "bad," and "egg." It is necessary for Burgess to achieve an empathic response to Alex, and these infantilisms within Nadsat are reminiscent of Dickensian innocence — serving well as buffer zones (or are they iron curtains?) between the "good" reader and the "evil" protagonist.

Other clues to this grim future world are Burgess's truncated and mechanized synecdoches: The "sarky guff" is a "sarcastic guffaw." "Pee and em" are Alex's parents; the "old in-out-in-out" is sexual intercourse (generally rape!); a "twenty-to-one" (the number is scarcely fortuitous) is a gang beating; "6655321" is Alex's prison name, and "StaJa 84" (State Jail 84) is his prison address.

Closely linked with the mechanical hybrids used in Nadsat are cer-tain words conspicuous by their absence. There are no words, for exam-ple, that give positive feelings of warmth or caring or love. When Alex wants to refer to goodness he has to do so by opting out of Nadsat and for English, or by calling evil "the other shop."

Yet the total effect of Nadsat is greater than the sum of its various parts. Alex, in the capacity of "Your Humble Narrator," uses the language to extrapolate a future both vague and too familiar. He sings of a time when all adults work, when very few read, and when society is middle class, middle-aged, and middle-bound. We are told only that 1960 is already history and that men are on the moon. The reader is offered no other assurances. And as the linguistic impact of Nadsat becomes more comprehensible, one is left to wonder if the world of clockwork oranges is so safely distant after all.

When one has truly and carefully followed the linguistic threads of Burgess's novel, the Minotaur guide can be heard arguing a matter deeply tragic in implications. By definition language, like its human author, man, has an essential right to reflect the fits and starts of a time-honed, familiar friend. There ought to be an ordered sense of choice, a spirit of chorus and harmony and solo. Jabberwocky is for fun; Nadsat is a very different construct and far more fearful. Though at times it can be beautiful, there is the lonely wail of tomorrow wrenched from the desperate sighs of today. In Nadsat one finds the Platonic form of mechanism: the cadence of a metronome and the ticking-tocking ramifications of humanity without its essence.

The deep and hard questions of *A Clockwork Orange,* however, are not veiled by the mechanical language. And standing richer when reviewed in light of the balance of Burgess's cosmogony, they stand even more specifically poignant when played against the panorama of all Burgess's writing. Through a reflective stage-setting, the reader is far more able to cope with the labyrinthine mind behind the dystopian clockwork.

Burgess is fond of envisioning himself as an exile. He has voluntarily absented himself from many situations with the voice of a vociferous (not a whimsical) outcast. He has politically removed his allegiances from Britain. He has removed himself from the aegis of the Catholic Church, voicing preference for a variety of heretical or mystical theologies. Burgess is truly a man of isolation, alone with his own thoughts and his fiction to espouse his maverick philosophy. The exclusive position that Burgess assumes lends his writing a metaphysically unique, if not philosophically original, dimension.

Locked within that mind — that mental labyrinth — is a most clever approach to serious metaphysical questions. Burgess has fashioned and shaped a dualist system of eclectic, authentic origin and pitted it against the world of the past, the present, and the future. Burgess's theological contentions are amazingly astute from the point of authenticity, universality, and relevance.

Much of his metaphysics is genuine philosophy given a fresh approach. He has drawn upon Eastern and Western philosophies, concocting a novel brew of Eastern dualism, heretical Manicheanism, Pelagian/Augustinianism, the cultural mythologies of ancient civilizations, the philosophy of Heraclitus, the implicit teachings of the Taoists, the Hegelian dialectic. The impact of Burgess's metaphysics, however, is not so much the clever jigsaw effect of a master eclectic; rather, it is that out of this syncretism Burgess has presented a serious allegory of the contemporary malaise, which has been diagnosed by all recent Existential and nihilistic thinking. He is answering through his writing the central paradoxes of life posed in Sartre's "nausea," Heidegger's "dread," and Kierkegaard's *Angst* and "fear and trembling."

Basically, twentieth-century man has come to live under the onerous speculations of recent philosophers. He has, in a sense, become a captive of his own (or what he used to feel was his own) universe. Ancient philosophers and artists were dedicated to the simple contention that the universe was a friendly home, divinely designed for mortal existence, and not incidentally mortal happiness. In varying degrees, yesterday's thinkers attempted to explain, rationalize, even challenge man's primacy upon earth; they seldom, however, questioned his right to be here or his natural relationship with the world in which he lived.

The last one hundred years saw the growing disaffiliation from the traditional acceptance of the world as benign. After thousands of years of philosophy dedicated to man's concentric sphere within the universe, nihilists and existentialists were now challenging not only man's place in the system but the entirety of the system itself. No longer was logic, or spirit, or mind, or even God the central force of the universe — these became only alternatives. The center of the universe was now existence; man's solitary life was enough just *in being*. Shockingly, this new paramount position of man left him not the conqueror of the universe but its victim. He was swamped by the very paradox that made his existence supreme. For in accepting and even reveling in the uniqueness of his own individuality, man was forced to accept that he was totally unnecessary. Adrift from the former Divine, or logical, or even scientific plan, adrift from Hegelian systems, humanity was presented with a position of supreme importance and, simultaneously, with the concept of its own total annihilation.

As the world more fully accepted that it was enough just to be, it became aware, too, that an individual existence, while central to that individual, was as nothing in the universe. With World War II and the prospect of total annihilation (not thousands, but millions of deaths and the promise of even greater debacle), the "nausea," "dread," and "fear" that had haunted the ivory towers of philosophers became a part of every living being.

Into this anxiety-ridden arena came the literature that chronicled, prescribed, and diagnosed a series of ways in which man could come to live with relative peace within himself. Yet always the paradox remained: each individual was a unique and single existence that had never been before and would never be again. Yet that same individual existence was nothing. It would die, never return, and the world would go on as before.

Burgess, for good or ill, has generally refused to enter the arena. Indeed, he has steered clear of the mainstream of the philosophical split alluded to above. He has removed himself as thoroughly and totally from this particular dialogue as he has from church and country. He is to be sure a chronicler of paradox. He, too, speaks and writes of polarity, ambiguity, juxtaposition. He does not, however, revile them; on the contrary — and this is perhaps what makes him unique among writers today — he seems to glory in them. Burgess's writing is dedicated to exposing the totality of the paradox and offering humanity an alternative to "fear and trembling." In a single shibboleth, Burgess demands that man first become aware of the paradoxes of life *and then accept them.* The injunction is neither so simplistic nor so naïve as it may at first appear.

Burgess offers his readers a cosmogony spinning in exact parallel to their own world. Yet, rather than trembling in the face of paradox, Burgess's cosmogony is energized by it. One is not at all surprised to find living side by side in *The Wanting Seed* "Mr. Live Dog" and "Evil God." "God" and "Not God" thrive in *Tremor of Intent,* and the following references from *A Clockwork Orange* show how energetic such dualisms can become:

> Hell and blast you all, if all you bastards are on the side of the Good, then I'm glad I belong to the other shop.

> But, brothers, this biting of their toe-nails over what is the *cause* of badness is what turns me into a fine laughing malchick. They don't go into what is the cause of *goodness,* so why of the other shop? If lewdies are good that's because they like it, and I wouldn't ever interfere with their pleasures, and so of the other shop.

Burgess advocates a pure dualism, reflected variously on earth as "X and Y," "left and right," "black and white," or "lewdies good and lewdies not good." The names and terms change with each novel, but the concepts are serious, unswerving, and consistent—head-to-head combat between equal but opposite deities who are the forces behind creation.

Although Burgess does not shout innuendos from the novel's lectern, he does posit dualism as a means for explaining the unexplainable. Garnered from the fiction itself—for Burgess has never formally outlined his philosophy—the dualistic system works something like this:

Each of the two divinities created a sphere. The "Good God" created an ascendant, ethereal sphere. It became a world of light, and summer, and warmth. Contrarily, the "Evil God" set his stage. His was a descendant sphere of darkness and winter cold. Thus the spinning universe contained the dual divinity and a massive panoramic background. One, the "Bog of the Good," all "gorgeousness and gorgeosity made flesh," gave to man a spirit, while the "God of the other shop" gave man his flesh—again, juxtaposition, ambiguity, paradox, and the need to choose.

The first and primary symbols of the Burgess cosmogony are the sun and moon. They are the mystical, mythical avatars that preside over the choosing upon the earth. Their qualities, both natural and allegorical, are the parameters of Burgess's fiction. Certain secondary symbols are, however, equally important for directing the protagonists' literal, as well as spiritual movement. From the partial list below, one can discern the two opposing spheres that directly relate to Burgess's dualistic universe, and the limbo sphere between them.

White ("Good God")	*Gray* ("Man")	*Black* ("Evil God")
sun	earth	moon
day	dawn/dusk	night
birth	life	death
creation	existence	destruction
grace	ambivalence	sin
past	present	future
soul	mind	body
summer	spring/fall	winter

Burgess uses this highly Manichean and dualistic world for most of his principal settings. His protagonists are allowed to live out their lives until the moment they are embodied in the novels. That moment becomes the moment of choice, and Burgess forces them to exercise the dualistic option. This aspect of choosing and "the choice" mark every plot and direct

protagonists from *A Vision of Battlements* to *The Napoleon Symphony*.
A novel like *MF* is (if one might forgive Burgess's own pun) riddled with
choices. *A Clockwork Orange,* however, is unique of aspect in that
Burgess is not working on a multiplicity of levels but concentrating on the
nature of choice which, by definition, must be *free*. To underscore his
message, Burgess is far more translucent about his symbolism in *A Clockwork Orange* than in most of his other novels.

The moon and the night and the winter are Alex's arena. Burgess has
always attached allegorical significance to the night and never more
heavily than here:

> The day was very different from the night. The night belonged
> to me and my droogs and all the rest of the nadsats, and the
> starry bourgeois lurked indoors drinking in the gloopy world-
> casts; but the day was for the starry ones and there always
> seemed to be more rozzes or millicents about during the day.

Scattered throughout the first section of the novel are innumerable
references to the night as the time of evil. ("The Luna was up" and "it was
winter trees and dark.") On Alex's final night raid that ends in death,
treachery, and incarceration, Burgess is continually outlining in black
and white:

> So we came nice and quiet to this domy called the Manse, and
> there were globe lights outside on iron stalks . . . and there was
> a light like dim on in one of the rooms on the ground level, and
> we went to a nice patch of street dark. . . . They [the droogs]
> nodded in the dark. . . . Then we waited again in darkness.

Burgess continues the imagery—the black of the evening, the light from
the windows, the white old woman, the pouring of white milk, the theft
of a white statue of Beethoven. Nearly blinded by the most stupid of his
droogs (significantly named Dim), Alex is captured by the police,
brought through the black night to the white of the police station: "They
dragged me into this very bright-lit whitewashed cantora."

Throughout the remainder of the novel Burgess employs a seemingly
confused pattern of white and black. The white-jacketed doctors are evil,
and as extreme versions of B. F. Skinner's behaviorists and advocates of
"the Ludovico technique," understandably so. In their hands (or rather in
their mechanical toils), Alex will become a clockwork orange: a piece of
pulpless, juiceless flesh that acts upon command and not out of will.
Conversely, the chaplain is a drunk garbed in black, yet he is the only

character within the novel who honestly questions the morality of this application of behavioral science.

The white of the doctors, the black of the prison cell, the white of the technicians, the black of the chaplain, the white of the interrogation room, the black of Alex's reentry into society — all are carefully balanced inversions. The reader has often to unravel such inversions — to work, that is, in and out of the maze — particularly within scenes with institutional settings. The same sorts of inversion occur in *The Doctor Is Sick* and in the hospital scenes from *Honey for the Bears*. Burgess generally inverts his black-white imagery in situations where the morality and ethics are prescribed and not chosen. Schools, prisons, military installations, and hospitals — all places calling for Burgess's use of color imagery — underscore, through studied inversion, his perception of a morally inverted, indeed perverted world.

In *A Clockwork Orange* Burgess has crafted a childmachine, placed him in the pit of tomorrow, and "voiced" him with the lament of a world so mesmerized by technocracy that it has lost its essence. Alex chooses to sin and the world cannot live with his choice. Dystopia takes away neither his sin nor his existence, but does take away his right to choose, and thereby his soul:

> Badness is of the self, the one, the you or me on our oddy knockies, and that self is made by old Bog or God and is his great pride and radosty. But the not-self cannot have the bad, meaning they of the government and the judges and the schools cannot allow the bad because they cannot allow the self. And is not our modern history, my brothers, the story of brave malenky selves fighting these big machines?

Alex does what he wants to do, so the world takes away his freedom to choose. He becomes a programmed good machine and no longer a person. Yet there has to be room for freedom, for by design this is a world of man. We are all "malenky selves on our oddy knockies" and the price of freedom runs high. We are a medial element, both desperate and sublime, with our *only* distinction being our right to choose. The paradox is one of enormity, for the stakes are enormous; the only alternative is of a mechanized hell.

Oddly enough, Burgess as man and as writer is caught in the same paradox he espouses. The mind does not journey far from the body; the medial element, the victimized chooser of Burgess's fictions, is really Burgess himself. The spirit as well as the body yearns for a place, a time to belong. The Far East, England, Malta, are all bridges he has burned behind him. Burgess has, through his fiction, his journalism, his determined stand, cut himself off in principle and in fact from much that he intellectually abhors yet emotionally loves. His church and his country go on, despite his verbal assaults. Like Gulliver, he might indeed be genuinely amazed that his satire of the human condition has not brought about immediate improvement of it. But then, like Swift—who, too, looks *down* to observe human nature, rather than *around*—he has been forced to pay for his olympian vision.

And, unfortunately, for his prophetic vision as well. Burgess's fiction is more alive today than even in the times it was written. One reads with amazement, if not ideed horror, that Burgess's prophecy has become fact. Zoroaster and Manes are dust now. Dualism is little more than an Eastern etiquette, permeating the life-style of Asia. Kierkegaard, Nietzsche, and Sartre are classics, venerable promulgators of the *Angst* and *nausée* that all of us have subliminally absorbed. But the dualistic paradox still continues to unwind itself, and we still throb in our gray cocoons, daring ourselves to opt for emergence into the day or into the night. Burgess would draw us out of ourselves and make us choose, would make us commit ourself to choice for choice's sake. Like Alex, we may become mere mechanism, or all will, incarnated in flesh and blood: a clockwork, or an orange. The responsibility is of course ours, and Burgess brilliantly instructs us how to shoulder the responsibility.

ROBERT MARTIN ADAMS

Joycean Burgess

Another fringe-Joycean is Anthony Burgess, who has written so many novels so fast that one is limited, for sheerly practical reasons, to mentioning only a couple of them. The Joyce-presence in Burgess is mostly linguistic, and perhaps beyond that musical; like Joyce, and like no other novelist in English, Burgess is fond of using language harmonically or impressionistically, and not just in nostalgic moods — he likes to strip words of their representational values and use them for their tonal values. This was apparent almost from the beginning. Without its special dialect, *A Clockwork Orange* would be not only a sparse but a muddled book, with its bare bones in evident disarray. There is a *1984* or *Brave New World* component in the book, a totalitarian society savagely conditioning its subjects into conformity; there is the urban gang-leader as outlaw-hero, a slummy Robin Hood; and there is Alex's particular hangup on classical music, which balances uncertainly in the middle of things — one moment a barbaric incitement to indiscriminate violence (in the rape of the two pre-adolescent ptitsas), one moment a nobler and more civilized vision, which is contaminated and degraded by being associated with violence. As a matter of fact, the whole conditioning experiment which is the center of the novel is unconvincing, because it consists of giving Alex a representational overdose of what he obviously enjoys in everyday life, sadistic cruelties. (One is not convinced that — even with the help of drugs — the movies he's forced to see would revolt him; there's just as good a

From *Afterjoyce: Studies in Fiction after Joyce.* ©1977 by Robert Martin Adams. Oxford University Press, 1977.

chance that they'd incite him.) In any case, having set up his alternatives —
Alex *au naturel,* a bloodthirsty guttersnipe, versus Alex brainwashed, a
whiny, sanctimonious guttersnipe — Burgess clearly was unable to resolve
them, and so bundled his novel toward an inconclusive ending.

But the dialect of the novel performs several services for this rather
crude fable. Being relatively opaque, it absorbs a lot of attention in its
own right; it's a rich mixture of Russian conflated with English, Romany,
rhyming slang, and Burgess-coinages, so that initially a lot of the meanings have to be guessed from the contexts. The reader is thus kept well oc-
cupied, not to say distracted; a good deal of his attention goes simply to
the surface of the novel. Reading the book also involves a lot of back-and-
forthing — that is, a word used in one context is given further meaning by
its use in another context further on, which reflects back on its first usage.
All this to-do on the linguistic surface of things blurs one's attention to
the overall shape of the novel, and the scenes of gleeful sadism work to re-
inforce that desirable superficiality. It's a flat novel written in a thick, im-
pasto style. The theme of music is integral to the novel, defined in this
way; it makes for tonal unity on an immediate and impressionistic level,
which is just another way of saying that the book is put together more like
a movie than like a novel.

It is also a book, like those of Joyce, largely unconcerned with
morality in any form. No doubt this was part of the reason for its popular
success; it was an authentically cold book, at which a reader was entitled
to shiver. Partly this was because of the society that Burgess envisioned,
but partly also it derived from a personal artistic option within the book.
One can almost feel the pathetic, beseeching figure of Poetic Justice im-
ploring the novelist for admittance to his book and being roughly
shouldered away. The writer whose book gives its title to Burgess's, whose
house was vandalized and whose wife was raped by Alex and his droogs, is
later allowed to play the samaritan to beaten Alex, and to suspect who it
is that he's helping, but never to know it. The "brothers" to whom the
story is recited are never identified, but we are bound to assume they are a
new set of droogs of whom Alex, now a casehardened pro, has become or
will become the leader. Droogery is thus unrebuked, even triumphant; if
only by contrast with the alternatives, its appeal is allowed.

Music in this novel which slants across all the categories, doesn't
work in any logical way on the narration, nor is it an integral part of the
plot, yet it's no less functional. In conjunction with the language, which
is a major source of the book's vitality, it suggests a sphere of instinctual
and uncorrupted response, such as neither *1984* nor *Brave New World*

ventures to represent, and which contrasts with the asphalt jungle of the book itself. It's this intimation of the primeval and healthy barbaric, if only as a possibility within the corrupt, sick barbaric of the city slumster, that's distinctively Burgess and at the same time strongly Joycean.

Even more marked is the application of Joycean prose in a pure entertainment like *Tremor of Intent*. Burgess, like Joyce, is delighted by the linguistic patterns that form in the fading shadows of unconsciousness; and in this wholly implausible thriller, the most impressive and inventive passages are those where various characters (Hillier, Roper, Theodorescu, and a Russian NKVD agent) wander off for one reason or another into gaga-land, letting words, their sounds, and their associations take over for the common order of discourse, or imposing on them a whole new order of non-meanings:

> I was not surprised. In a way I was pleased [writes Roper]. My sense of betrayal was absolute. I fetched the barnaby out of the cheese-slice, fallowed the whereupon with ingrown versicles, then cranked with endless hornblows of white, gamboge, wortdrew, harimon, and prayrichard the most marvellous and unseen-as-yet fallupons that Old Motion ever hatched in all his greenock nights.

We couldn't, perhaps, take this wamble-speech in extended and uninterrupted doses, and Burgess doesn't give us a great deal of it. Even the Clockwork Orange dialect runs down perceptibly in the latter part of that novel, and the freakyspeak in *Tremor of Intent* is even more carefully spotted than that. Still, though it's only a dash of Joycean seasoning on books which are of a pretty common order, Burgess unmistakably uses that garnish, and not by any means to contemptible effect. Where Durrell escapes *from* Joycean structure in the course of the Alexandria novels, Burgess at the high point of his fictions escapes *into* Joycean language. The one author is no more interested in palimpsest effects, narrative discontinuities, and classical analogues, than the other is in twilight states of consciousness; neither has much of a hand for parody, neither is a self-vivisector. Both are entertainers, and in that capacity both are willing to settle for varieties of short-range effect that come close to claptrap — *coups de théâtre* with suave, ice-cold heavies and sultry, fire-lipped temptresses — all suffused with the aroma of musty theatrical trunks, from which they were just dragged. To point out that elements of Joyce served authors of this character is not to add very much to his permanent glory on the Homer-Dante-Flaubert scale, but it humanizes and facilitates him, suggesting the dimensions and directions of his work that were most readily domesticated. In neither case is there any question of pushing Joyce's work further than he himself carried it; on the contrary, Burgess and Durrell use only one aspect apiece of the Joycean enterprise, and handle it very gingerly in their own novels. Yet for the most part, that salt is what gives the rest of the dish its savor.

GEOFFREY AGGELER

Pelagius and Augustine

A desire to ascertain the "liberalism" or "conservatism" of writers who have provided us with significant commentaries on human experience is frequently an efficient cause of much of the critical exegesis of their works. In the case of many of the most significant commentators—Shakespeare and Conrad, for example—the issue can never be resolved. They transcend any possibility of categorization in these terms, no matter how the terms are limited or applied. Shakespeare and Conrad have both been termed "aristocratic" and "politically conservative" in their attitudes, but the adherence of these labels, or their opposites, must depend upon a selective reading of their works. Although none of Shakespeare's works could reasonably be termed antiaristocratic, it is nonetheless clear that he has illuminated fallacies underlying aristocratic attitudes and values. Coriolanus's personal magnificence and his apt comments on "the mutable rank-scented many" must be balanced against his willful blindness and the folly bred into him as an aristocrat. Similarly, Conrad's observations on the futility of revolution in his preface to *Under Western Eyes* must be balanced against more "liberal" observations in his essay "Autocracy and War."

So it is with Burgess. The temptation to label him in these terms is especially strong because so many of the conflicts in his novels are between Pelagian liberals and Augustinian conservatives. By his use of these terms, Burgess intends to remind us of the ultimate origins of much of

From *Anthony Burgess: The Artist as Novelist.* © 1979 by the University of Alabama Press.

the so-called liberalism and conservatism in Western thinking. In Burgess's view, the liberal's optimism, his belief in the fundamental goodness and perfectability of man, derives from an ancient heresy — the Pelagian denial of original sin. Not surprisingly, he believes the doctrinal bases of much of the pessimism pervading Western conservative thinking can be traced to Augustine's well-known refutations of Pelagian doctrine. In view of the frequency of clashes between Pelagians and Augustinians in Burgess's fiction, it is worthwhile to review their principal differences.

THE SEMINAL DEBATE

Pelagius, a British monk who resided in Rome, Africa, and Palestine during the early decades of the fourth century, set forth doctrines concerning human potentiality that virtually denied the necessity of Divine Grace and made the redemption a superfluous gesture. Such an assault on basic Christian doctrine does not, however, seem to have been part of his original design. What he sought to promote initially was an awakening of Christians from the sinful indolence into which they had fallen, largely, he thought, as a result of underestimating their spiritual potentialities as human beings. He believed that just as the Roman ideal of preeminent heroic virtue, embodied in the term *virtus,* was attainable by any Roman who applied himself, so the Christian ideal was attainable by any Christian through his own efforts, using his own natural gifts. If this were not the case, how could we account for the virtuous, self-denying lives of the pagan philosophers? What about the Patriarchs? What about Job? The fact that they were able to please God without the explicit guidance of the Torah is indisputable evidence of the natural goodness of humanity. It cannot be denied of course that the evidence of man's innate goodness became less plentiful after the time of the Patriarchs, but this, in Pelagius's view, would explain the necessity of the explicit revelation of God's law. The law, hitherto unnecessary, was revealed to guide men back to the path of righteousness that their forefathers had followed by natural inclination.

It is not surprising that Grace, in its most widely accepted orthodox sense, as an infusion of the Holy Spirit, did not occupy a very prominent place in the Pelagian scheme of salvation. Pelagius likened it to a sail attached to a rowboat in which the oars, the only essential means of locomotion, might be likened to the human will. The sail makes rowing easier, but the boat could reach its destination without it: "*Velo facilius, remo difficilius: tamen et remo itur.*" In short, as W. J. Sparrow-Simpson observes, "Grace in the sense of supernatural strength imparted is obviously superfluous in the Pelagian view." Man rows the boat, and by his own unaided exertion on the oars, he merits God's approval.

Pelagius's cavalier treatment of Divine Grace was a concomitant of his total rejection of orthodox doctrines concerning original sin: "Everything good and everything evil, in respect of which we are either worthy of praise or of blame, is *done by us,* not *born with us.*" He and his less discreet disciple Coelestius were also condemned for teaching that Adam's sin injured no one but himself and that he would have been mortal whether he had sinned or not. His sin has no effect on new-born infants, who are in the same spiritual condition that Adam was in before the Fall. Since they are in a state of prelapsarian innocence, they may attain eternal life even without baptism. Moreover, just as it was not through Adam's sin that men became mortal, so it is not through Christian resurrection that they may have life beyond the grave. The fact that men such as Job and the Patriarchs had led sinless lives before Christ's coming indicated that the law, as well as the gospel, could lead men to God's kingdom.

Augustine was horrified by these teachings. Recognizing them as essentially an abandonment of Christianity itself, he devoted fully as much energy to discrediting them as he had previously given to refuting the Manichees. In mounting his attack, he relied heavily upon scripture, especially the Epistles of St. Paul, but his fervor and the intensity of his insistence on the helplessness and fundamental wickedness of man without Divine Grace cannot be accounted for simply in terms of his objective appreciation of the soundness of Pauline doctrine. Clearly, he was also moved by the memory of his own early slavery to sin, which he describes so vividly in the *Confessions.* In these spiritual memoirs, he looked back with bitter revulsion at his wanton, aimless youth when he was motivated only by vanity and appetite and, contrary to all fashionable moral theory, capable of delighting in evil for its own sake: "Foul soul, falling from Thy firmament to utter destruction; not seeking aught through the shame, but the shame itself!" Without the Grace of Baptism and the assurance of Christ the Mediator's intercession, his damnation would have been assured. At one point, filled with a sense of his helplessness without Grace, he uttered a prayer that outraged Pelagius: "I have no hope at all but in thy great mercy. Grant what thou commandest and command what thou wilt."

In Augustine's view, it is impossible for any man to choose a path of righteousness without divine assistance. He has been created with freedom of choice and God's law has been revealed to him, but these gifts cannot save him unless he also receives the free gift of the Holy Spirit, the Grace "whereby there arises in his soul the delight in and the love of God, the supreme and changeless Good." Without this divine infusion and the accompanying delight in pleasing God, an awareness of the law serves only to accelerate one's progress toward damnation, for it merely increases one's desire for whatever it has prohibited and fills him with the guilt of transgression when he yields to the desire. Moreover, if a man obeys the law out of fear or any motive other than the love of God, he has done nothing meritorious. Augustine found the whole question of the relationship of the law to Divine Grace summarized in St. Paul's text, "the letter killeth, but the Spirit giveth life." This dictum might be taken to mean that literal interpretations should not be enforced upon the figurative sayings of scripture. But it must also be taken to mean "that the letter of the law, admonishing us to avoid sin, kills, if the life-giving Spirit be not present. . . . The apostle's aim is to commend the grace which came through Jesus Christ to all peoples, lest the Jews exalt themselves above the rest on account of their possession of the law." Had there been no redemption, there could be no justification. If, as the Pelagians say, men can achieve salvation simply by exerting their natural gifts in conformity with the law, then, as St. Paul says, "Christ has died for nought."

Man's feeble condition, in Augustine's opinion, was not any basis for complaint about the justice of the Creator. The origin of evil itself, he argued, could be located in the free will of rational creatures, and man's total culpability for sin could be explained in terms of original sin. God, it is true, created man's nature, but we must realize that as a result of the Fall, there are essentially two types of human condition that may be designated by the expression *human nature*. There is (or rather was) the condition of prelapsarian innocence in which man, as created, had complete freedom and ability to pursue the path of righteousness. As a result of Adam's sin, however, human nature has been vitiated and corrupted. This latter condition, a "penal" state in which man is impeded from pursuing righteousness by ignorance and an inability to overcome the urgings of his flesh, is also termed "human nature." Actually, we should restrict the expression to that state of innocence and freedom man enjoyed before the Fall. Man freely abandoned that condition, and, as he is now, lacks both freedom and goodness: "Because he is what he now is, he is not good, nor is it in his power to become good, either because he does not see what he ought to be, or, seeing it, has not the power to be what he sees he ought to be."

So much for the seminal debate. If we are willing to share Burgess's vision and set aside, or at least look beyond, the narrowly theological aspects of it and view "Augustinian" and "Pelagianism" in terms of their broad philosophical implications, we can see that the council of Carthage in A.D. 418, which condemned Pelagianism, was by no means the end of it. The debate has in fact continued in the West with periodically varying degrees of intensity down to our own time. Its more vigorous sessions include the fourteenth-century clash between Bradwardine and Ockham and the conflict three centuries later between the Jansenists and the Jesuits. Outstanding Augustinian spokesmen include Luther, Calvin, Jansen, Pascal, Racine, Hobbes, Swift, and Edmund Burke. Some of the more notable Pelagians are Shaftesbury, Corneille, Hume, Rousseau, Jefferson, Thomas Paine, Marx, Hegel, John Stuart Mill, Edward Bellamy, and most of the major English and German romantic poets. The validity of these classifications depends of course upon a willingness to view the debate in terms of its social and political as well as its religious implications.

When the debate is viewed in broader terms, the nature of man emerges as the pivotal issue, and one can see that the diametrically opposed assumptions of Augustine and Pelagius could be take as premises of diametrically opposed political philosophies as well as attitudes toward social progress as far removed as hope and despair. The Pelagian view of humanity justifies optimism and a Rousseauvian trust in *la volonté générale* (the general will). Indeed if one could accept Pelagius's sanguine estimates of human potentiality, one might hope to see Heaven on earth. For surely, if men can achieve spiritual perfection and merit external salvation solely through the use of their natural gifts, the solutions to all problems of relations within earthly society must be well within their grasp. They need only to be enlightened properly, and their fundamental goodness will inevitably incline them toward morally desirable social goals. The realization of a universally acceptable utopia would not depend upon the imposition of any particular social structure. Rather, humanity, if properly enlightened, could be trusted to impose itself a utopian social scheme.

To say the least, there is a good deal less hope implied in Augustine's doctrines than in Pelagius's. One can readily see that Augustine's fundamentally pessimistic view of human potentiality, his basic distrust of human nature, could be taken as the basis of policies of rigorous enforcement in human affairs. A utopia organized upon Augustinian premises must necessarily be a police state and in this connection, it is certainly no accident that the human community most closely approximating such a

utopia was Geneva in the time of Calvin. Calvin, like Luther, relied very
heavily upon Augustine in the formulation and support of his doctrines,
and it would appear that the enormous importance he attached to the enforcement of discipline within the Christian community derived largely
from his fundamental agreement with the Augustinian view of human
nature.

Burgess's view of the debate encompasses its broadest implications,
and some awareness of these implications, especially within social and
political spheres of Western thinking, is essential to an appreciation of his
social satire. In *The Wanting Seed,* for instance, we are shown a fascist
police state of the future emerging from the ruins of a future socialist
democracy, and emerging with it are eager entrepreneurs, "rats of the
Pelphase but Augustine's lions." The full irony of this metaphor cannot
be grasped simply with reference to Augustinian doctrine in its pre-
Calvinist, pre-Gilded Age purity. Burgess intends to remind us of the
ways in which Augustinian/Calvinist doctrines on grace, election, and
unregenerate human nature have molded the socioeconomic ethics of
Calvin's intellectual and spiritual heirs both in the Old World and the
New. In this same novel and in his other proleptic nightmare, *A Clockwork Orange,* he also reveals some likely doctrinal developments of the
future. The forces that contend for governmental mastery are labeled
"Pelagian" and "Augustinian," but they are more obviously Rousseauvian
and Hobbesian. It is natural that their conflicting philosophies should
seem to echo *Leviathan, De Cive (The Citizen), Du Contrat Social (The
Social Contract),* and the *Discours sur l'inégalité (Discourse on the Origin
of Inequality),* rather than the treatises of Pelagius and Augustine, since
both novels are set in a future in which the issue of Divine Grace and indeed theology have been virtually forgotten. Augustinianism without
theology becomes Hobbism, and Pelagianism even in its original form
was not far removed from romantic primitivism. In short, Burgess's satiric
vision encompasses the entire debate—past, present, and future—and
one may find, especially in his dystopian books, echoes of the writings of
all participants I mentioned here and a good many more.

THE WANTING SEED

The Wanting Seed is Burgess's fullest and most explicit treatment of
the Augustinian/Pelagian conflict. In this Orwellian/Malthusian proleptic nightmare, he presents a cyclical theory of history—as essentially a
perpetual oscillation or "waltz" between two philosophical "phases"—a

Pelagian phase and an Augustinian. As the novel opens, we behold a
world in which our undernourished descendants have little more than
standing room. England, as suffocatingly crowded as the rest of the
world, is under the benevolent guidance of a "Pelagian" government.
Official attitudes and policies are, however, more distinctively Rousseauvian than Pelagian. Indeed, the shocking vision of the Malthusian nightmare itself may remind one of Jean-Jacques's pronouncement that "the
government under which, without external aids, without naturalization
of colonies, the citizens increase and multiply most is beyond question
the best." Just as the folly of this assumption is revealed, the incredible
naïveté of the Pelagian government's Rousseauvian political philosophy is
also revealed. According to Rousseau, "The general will [*La volonté
générale*] is always in the right, but the judgment that guides it is not
always informed"; hence it follows that laws must be provided, not as
restrictions, but as signposts pointing men toward the greatest common
good, the object of their natural inclinations. Burgess's sardine-can
civilization comes into being largely because the government has been
unshakable in its trust in *la volonté générale*. Despite massive proof to
the contrary, it maintains an optimistic belief that "the great liberal
dream seems capable of fulfillment." Coercion is officially eschewed.
Laws exist merely as guidelines to lead the cramped citizenry to "precise
knowledge of the total needs of the community." Since the official faith
dictates that a desire to act for the common good is a basic component of
human nature, "it is assumed that the laws will be obeyed" and that an
elaborate punitive system is unnecessary.

The fact that the economy is totally controlled by the state does not
indicate any official lack of trust in the people. On the contrary, it is
believed that without capitalism, the state is more securely subject to the
general will. Tristram Foxe, the history teacher-protagonist, informs his
pupils that as civilization approaches the liberal millenium, these tokens
are thought to be manifest:

> The sinful acquisitive urge is lacking, brute desires are kept
> under rational control. The private capitalist, for instance, a
> figure of top-hatted greed, has no place in Pelagian society.
> Hence the State controls the means of production, the State is
> the only boss. But the will of the State is the will of the citizen,
> hence the citizen is working for himself.

This is of course another feature of the society that would please Rousseau
and some of the other "Pelagians" mentioned above.

Pelagian faith is not, however, in itself the principal reason the world has become so cramped. Rather, this is a major factor in man's failure to deal realistically or responsibly with the main problem, which is his own procreative instinct. Because of man's failure to control his sperm, the world has become overpopulated beyond Malthus's most fearsome imaginings. All of Malthus's positive and preventive "checks" — through "misery," "vice," and "moral restraint" — are destined to be brought into play, and it is clearly demonstrated that even in England circumstances could make them much less distinguishable from each other than the good Anglican demographer had assumed.

During its Pelagian phase, England relies heavily upon what Malthus would call checks through "vice" and "improper arts." Homosexuality, castration, abortion, and infanticide are all encouraged by a desperate government. The Pelagian leaders share Malthus's belief that the educated classes can be persuaded by reason to act for the common good while the proletariat cannot. Hence, although the state makes little attempt to sway the "proles," it seeks to influence the more "responsible" classes by education, propaganda, and social pressure. Everywhere posters blare *"It's Sapiens to be Homo."* A "Homosex Institute" offers both day and evening classes. People are able to improve their social and economic positions only if they can maintain a reputation either of "blameless sexlessness" or nonfertile sexuality. The protagonist misses a deserved promotion because, as a superior tells him, "A kind of aura of fertility surrounds you, Brother Foxe." Among other things, Tristram has fathered a child, and, although each family is legally allowed one birth, "the best people just don't. Just don't." Necessity has thus completely inverted sexual mores, and whereas Malthus would have termed these measures checks through "vice" and "improper arts," this cramped society sees them as checks through "moral restraint."

Overpopulation is the main cause of this inversion, but clearly another important causative factor is the present-day liberal trend toward sympathy for the homosexual. Burgess has remarked that "the homosexual is on the rise in the west." If Western popular entertainment is a valid indicator, the point is hard to dispute. Movies such as *That Certain Summer, The Staircase,* and *A Taste of Honey* and television plays such as *Who's Art Morrison?* emphasize the warm humanity of homosexuals and the injustice of their being rejected by society. Popular singers, such as the Rolling Stones and Alice Cooper, whatever their personal sexual inclinations in fact, present images of sexual ambiguity, and their appeal may be accounted for partly in terms of it. The rigid, mutually exclusive classification of humanity into raw masculinity and ultrafemininity has been seen as a source of psychic disorder. Less popular entertainment, that is, serious literature, has of course always included some sympathetic presentations of homosexuality, but the sympathy, not to mention the example, of serious writers could never offer homosexuals generally the hope for acceptance that they may now enjoy. It takes no great imaginative exertion to see that if the homosexual's sexual bias could be found to be socially useful, something more than acceptance might follow. Indeed, his or her bias might well become a desired norm. If this seems far-fetched, it might be well to recall that the ancient Greeks were not faced with a comparable population explosion. Man's sexual mores, like his economic ethics, are extremely flexible and in a state of constant metamorphosis. The attitudes of medieval moralists toward concupiscence appear as quaint and rationally indefensible to us as their attitudes toward usury.

In spite of steadily diminishing rations and standing room, the Pelagian government remains committed to an official faith of optimism and progress that assumes citizens will be reasonable enough to modify their sexuality for the common good, and that they will do so more or less voluntarily. There is a large, well-trained, mostly epicene force of population police (the "Poppol") that discreetly encourages people to conform to official moral standards, but its role is more persuasive than coercive, at least until the advent of the great "DISAPPOINTMENT." Pelagian liberalism, as Tristam Foxe tells his pupils, inevitably breeds "DISAPPOINTMENT," and the government itself becomes vulnerable as soon as there is compelling evidence that people are more selfish than the official credo dictates they should be. The evidence becomes significant when basic appetitive needs are denied. Although the "best people" may be willing to unsex themselves or to rechannel their sexuality, not even the most public-spirited can transcend the need for food. The food shortage caused by irresponsible procreation is made even more severe by a worldwide scourge of blights and animal diseases.

The Pelagian government's official faith in man has necessitated an official denial of the existence of God, but this scourge has the all-encompassing character of an expression of divine wrath, and eventually even the Pelagian leaders are driven to prayer. In addition to praying, the government hastily organizes a rather brutish police auxiliary, the "greyboys" (who strongly resemble the *Gris* force employed by the Spanish civil government under Franco) to assist the Poppol in maintaining order. However, neither prayer nor a beefed-up police force can prevent the gruesome consequences of overpopulation. Without domestic animals, seafood, or edible crops, people turn to each other, and widespread cannibalism is the most ghastly aspect of the chaotic "Interphase" that follows the complete breakdown of Pelagian methods of civil control. People are murdered and devoured by anthropophagic "dining clubs." Frequently these cannibal feasts are followed by heterosexual orgies "in the ruddy light of the fat-spitting fires." Tristram, wandering about the countryside in search of his wife, occasionally takes part in both feasts and orgies. He also witnesses a fertility ritual strongly reminiscent of ancient Dionysian festivals and, not surprisingly, a rebirth of drama. Indeed, in some respects the Interphase brings refreshing improvements—freedom of religion (including some rather grisly bits of breadless "transubstantiation"), open heterosexual love, and a revival of folk culture.

But chaos, "indiscriminate cannibalism and the drains out of order" cannot long be borne by a whole society of once-civilized people. The time is ripe for a coup, and the "Augustinians" do not hesitate. Seizing the reins of government, they quickly create an army and restore order. They then deal with social problems in the light of what they consider to be a more realistic assessment of human nature. Unlike the Pelagians, they acknowledge the reality of sin and, like Augustine himself, they recognize it as an "abiding condition" in which a sizable percentage of their fellow men are hopelessly fixed by their very nature. Burgess labels these pessimistic reformers "Augustinians," but their cynicism and bottomless contempt for humanity are more Hobbesian (or perhaps Swiftian) than Augustinian. Certainly their impaired moral vision, resulting from their total preoccupation with social stability, reminds us more of Hobbes than of Augustine.

It soon appears that the experience of cannibalism has suggested to the Augustinian leaders new methods of achieving social stability. Essential to their scheme is a re-creation of war as it had been fought long before, during the twentieth century. As they see it, war can be both a social "drainage system" and a partial solution to the problem of hunger in an overpopulated world. Social misfits of one kind or another, male and female, are drafted into the army, trained in complete isolation from the rest of the population, and then shipped for extermination to carefully contrived "battlefields." The actual slaughtering method used is simply a contrived World War I-type battle in which ignorant armies go over the top and clash by night. In the typical "extermination session" witnessed by Tristram Foxe, male and female armies destroy each other completely. The remains are then gathered up to be processed in tins for human consumption. There is a widely held assumption that canning makes cannibalism a relatively civilized affair. "It makes all the difference," as one soldier tells Tristram, "if you get it out of a tin."

Only the government and civilian contractors know that the heroes are bound for this dismal Valhalla. The rest of the population, not unlike some of their ancestors, simply cheers them on, content to be totally ignorant of the objectives of the war, the character of the enemy, and the nature of the warfare devouring its soldiers. Understandably, the ruling class exhibits a Hobbesian annoyance at any attempt on the part of the soldiers or citizens to become informed or involved. Tristram receives a nearly fatal military assignment because he holds discussion with his men concerning the issues of the war in which they are involved and the nature of the enemy. The officer who makes the assignment obviously subscribes to the military ethic summarized in Stephen Decatur's famous toast to his country, but he also represents the Hobbesian attitude of the ruling class. In his *De Cive* (*The Citizen*), Hobbes specifically excludes moral assessments of governmental policy from the duties of citizenship, and in *Leviathan*, he draws wistful distinctions between well-ordered societies of insects and human societies in which there is always a troublesome tendency of citizens to seek involvement in their own government.

The "drainage system" and the rest of the government functions must of course be in the hands of responsible individuals, and in a latter-day "Augustinian," that is, neo-Calvinist or Hobbist, state, the most responsible individuals are directors of corporations. "Private enterprise," we are told, is the "beginning of Gusphase," and "election," that is, economic significance, is proven by efficient, functionally significant involvement in the military/industrial complex. In fact, the "War Department" itself is a corporation with a renewable charter. Its indisputable success in remedying previously insoluble problems makes its employees confident that the charter will be renewed perpetually. They believe that so long as there is an army to absorb "the morons and enthusiasts," "the ruffians, the perverts, the death-wishers," and the "cretinous [female] over-producers," it is possible to maintain "a safe and spacious community. A clean house full of happy people." There is a suggestion that the protagonist, like the man whose surname he shares, may chronicle the fate of exterminated martyrs to social stability, but one gathers that such a chronicle would accomplish little toward accelerating the advent of a new Pelagian phase. As the example of Nazi Germany suggests, in a well-fed, martially involved "clean house full of happy people" citizens *are* apt to look the other way and close their nostrils to the smell of burning flesh.

Parenthetically, in connection with this last point, we can perhaps see another reason why Burgess relegates capitalism to Gusphase. The militaristic Augustinian society with its acceptance of (if not indifference to) mass murder for the sake of social stability obviously resembles Nazi Germany, and it is generally agreed that Hitler's rise would have been much less meteoric without the help of Bolshevik-fearing industrialists. It may also be remembered that some imaginative German entrepreneurs fattened their purses designing and building camps, and even during the last years of the Third Reich profits were still being made by those who could design the special pitch forks, ovens, and other appliances needed to facilitate a stepped-up extermination process. This seems to be the sort of "civilian contractor" Burgess has in mind.

The Wanting Seed concludes on a note that may or may not be optimistic. We see the Pelagian prime minister, surrounded by his catamites, enjoying a pleasant exile in a seaside villa, calculating the moment of his return to power. But even more significant than his personal optimism is the optimism of scientists who are forging ahead in their efforts to locate nonanthropophagic sources of food. They are preparing to ferret them out in the abysmal depths of the sea: "Untouched life lurked, miles down, leagues down." Successful conquests of natural elements encourage a belief in man's ability to control nature completely and a concomitant belief that man can control himself by an exercise in reason. The advent of another Pelagian phase may be delayed, but it will come. The "waltz" never ceases.

The great drama of the "waltz" itself is the main focus of the novel, but we are also shown some of its effects on particular individuals, especially the history-teacher protagonist. His given name emphasizes with heavy irony the nonheroic quality of this future age. Like Tristram of old, he embarks on a quest that carries him throughout much of England, but there the resemblance ends. Instead of cuckolding his uncle, he is himself cuckolded by his brother. Instead of hacking and thrusting his way to immortal martial glory, he has the distinction of being the only soldier to escape an "extermination session" and entombment as canned meat. There is irony, too, in that he is a historian whose understanding of the "waltz" is more complete than that of any other character in the novel. For all his understanding of historic process, he is tossed about helplessly, unable to control his own destiny in any way until he flees the battlefield. In one sense, he does illustrate the idea of Marx and Hegel that man's freedom depends upon, indeed consists in, his awareness of some inevitable historic process. In another, he contradicts these great Pelagians who saw in "man's" growing awareness cause for optimism. Tristram's awareness, which is large to begin with and increases considerably, gives neither him nor us much cause for optimism since it leads him only to foresee endless repetitions of the cycle and no static millenium.

History teachers are not the only ones who understand the cycle. Consummate Machiavellian bureaucrats, such as Tristram's treacherous brother Derek, adapt chameleonlike to the moral standards officially promoted during each phase and thrive. During Pelphase, Derek — his name suggests cold-blooded support — is impeccably epicene. No one except a not-too-bright, would-be rival even suspects he is cuckolding his brother. Tristram's wife, Beatrice-Joanna, also has a suggestive name, and in a novel as full of comic/ironic literary allusions as this one, we have much to gain by following hints. Beatrice-Joanna is the name of the passionate heroine in Thomas Middleton's best-known play *The Changeling*. The term *changeling* can refer to a child or thing substituted by stealth, especially an elf child left by fairies. Derek, the Machiavellian pseudo-fairy, unintentionally impregnates his sister-in-law and thereby substitutes his own offspring for Tristram's child, whom she has recently lost. This piece of Pelagian bad luck is very much to his advantage later on during the "Gusphase" when it is important for rising bureaucrats to prove their heterosexuality and potency. He rises quite as rapidly in the Augustinian Ministry of Fertility as he had previously risen in the Pelagian Ministry of Infertility.

Although these characters are certainly far from being Burgess's subtlest psychological studies, they serve admirably to convey his ideas in a novel that is a major contribution to the subgenre known as the dystopian "novel of ideas." Surprisingly, the novel's initial critical reception was not terribly enthusiastic. That is, although some reviewers were and are enthusiastic, the book seems to have antagonized the more influential critics. Brigid Brophy, for one, termed it "half-baked." Another critic, assessing it more favorably, considered it "heavy-handed" as a piece of satire. In fact, a careful reading of *The Wanting Seed* fails to support either of these hyphenated strictures, and one is tempted to wonder about the extent to which this novel's unfavorable reception was caused by an awareness that it had been produced in some haste along with several others. The novel's only significant weakness proceeds from Burgess's tendency to be too entertaining and too witty. (Although he didn't wish to apply it, W. H. Pritchard's phrase "debilitating cleverness" is well chosen.) The novel is full of playful references to Burgess's fellow novelists and other literary figures. There is, for example, the description of the bearded giant atop the Government Building, which is identified from time to time with various figures of cultural and political importance, including "Eliot (a long dead singer of sterility)." The reports of cannibalism include the account of how "a man called Amis suffered savage amputation of an arm off Kingsway," and how "S. R. Coke, journalist, was boiled in an old copper near Shepherd's Bush; Miss Joan Waine, a teacher, was fried in segments." In themselves, these allusions and fantasies are delightful, but they combine with occasional flippancies of tone to deprive the book of some of its potential impact. As with the black-comic film classic *Dr. Strangelove,* the hilarity of presentation occasionally tends to make it difficult to bear in mind the seriousness of the themes.

Excessive hilarity is not, however, a ruinous weakness, either in *Strangelove* or *The Wanting Seed.* Ours is an age in which gallows humor is invaluable as a safeguard of our sanity, and as one reads the dark comedies of Burgess, Evelyn Waugh, Nabokov, and more recent "black-comic" effusions, such as Romain Gary's *The Dance of Genghis Cohn,* Kurt Vonnegut's *Cat's Cradle,* or even Gore Vidal's scabrous *Myra Breckinridge,* one must be impressed by the soundness of Thomas Mann's observations on modern tragedy and comedy in the preface to his translation of Conrad's *The Secret Agent.* Mann felt that "broadly and essentially, the striking feature of modern art is that it has ceased to recognize the categories of tragic and comic, or the dramatic classifications, tragedy and comedy, with the result that the grotesque is its most genuine style — to the extent, indeed, that today that is the only guise in which the sublime may appear."

The Wanting Seed is, in Mann's sense, a "grotesque" drama, and, like Shakespeare's sonnets, it is a relatively late but fresh and enduring contribution to a subgenre that seemed to have been worked to death. It antagonized some influential critics but is greatly admired by more youthful intellectuals, especially in America, who see in it a book that passes the test of "relevance," not merely because it depicts some possible consequences of the population explosion we all fear, but also because it gives a horribly convincing picture of the alternatives modern man may face at some time in the near future in his endless quest for social stability: If he isn't, in one sense or another, "eaten" by a military-industrial complex, he will be persuaded to castrate himself, in one way or another, for the sake of social stability.

A CLOCKWORK ORANGE

Even before Stanley Kubrick's brilliant and faithful rendering of *A Clockwork Orange* in film, this was probably Burgess's most widely read novel. This does not greatly please Burgess, who values some of his other novels much more. Like *The Wanting Seed,* it is a proleptic nightmare with dystopian implications. Although it can be read as an answer to and a rejection of the main ideas of B. F. Skinner, the author of such works as *Walden Two* and *Beyond Freedom and Dignity,* Burgess seems to have been directly influenced less by Skinner's ideas in particular than by accounts he had read of behaviorist methods of reforming criminals that were being tried in American prisons with the avowed purpose of limiting the subjects' freedom of choice to what society called "goodness." This struck Burgess as "most sinful," and his novel is, among other things, an attempt to clarify the issues involved in the use of such methods.

The setting of *A Clockwork Orange* is a city somewhere in either western Europe or North America where a civilization has evolved out of a fusion of the dominant cultures east and west of the Iron Curtain. This cultural merger seems to be partly the result of successful cooperative efforts in the conquest of space, efforts that have promoted a preoccupation with outer space and a concomitant indifference to exclusively terrestrial affairs such as the maintenance of law and order in the cities. As it does in *The Wanting Seed,* Pelagian faith in *A Clockwork Orange* also accompanies Promethean fire. Appropriately, there is shop looting on Gagarin Street, an avenue of this Western metropolis, and a victim of teenaged hoodlums is moved to ask, "What sort of a world is it at all? Men on the moon and men spinning around the earth like it might be midges round a lamp, and there's not no attention paid to earthly law nor order no more."

In light of recent events, a reader is apt to assume Burgess was thinking of the United States when he envisioned this situation of the future. In fact, he was more directly influenced by what he had seen during his visit to Leningrad in 1961. At that time, Russia was leading in the space race, and the gangs of young thugs called "stilyagi" were becoming a serious nuisance in Russian cities. At the same time, London police were having their troubles with the young toughs known as the "teddy boys." Having seen both the stilyagi and the teddy boys in action, Burgess was moved by a renewed sense of the oneness of humanity, and the murderous teenaged hooligans who are the main characters in *A Clockwork Orange* are composite creations. Alex, the fifteen-year-old narrator-protagonist, could be either an Alexander or an Alexei. The names of his three comrades in mischief, Dim, Pete, and Georgie, are similarly ambiguous, suggesting both Russian and English given names.

A reader may miss these and other hints completely but what he cannot overlook is the effect of culture fusion on the teenage underworld patois in which the story is narrated. The language itself, Burgess's invention, is called *nadsat,* which is simply a transliteration of a Russian suffix equivalent to the English suffix *teen,* as in "fifteen." Most, although by no means all, the words comprising nadsat are Russian, and Burgess has altered some of them in ways that one might reasonably expect them to be altered in the mouths of English-speaking teenagers. There is, for instance, the word *horrorshow,* a favorite adjective of nadsat speakers meaning everything from "good" to "splendid." The word sounds like a clever invention by an observer of teenagers who is aware of their fondness for films such as *I Was a Teenage Werewolf* and *Frankenstein Meets the Wolfman.* Actually it is an imagined development from *kharashó,* a Russian adjective meaning "good" or "well." The initial consonant, an unvoiced velar fricative (IPA/x/), is nonexistent in English, and the supposition that it would become a voiceless glottal fricative in the mouths of British or American teenagers is quite in accord with phonetic probability, since the aspirate is already contained in the Russian phoneme. This is not to say that *horrorshow* is purely the result of phonemic or phonetic change. Juvenile fondness for cinematic shockers has obviously had something to do with it and has indeed modified the Russian word further by adding new associations. Something that is "good" in the view of these young savages is something that thrills or shocks, like a film about Dracula. Well-delivered blows ("tolchocks") to the head or groin, fast cars, and ample female bosoms are more than "good"; they're "horrorshow."

A similar "loanshift" can be seen in the nadsat word *rabbit,* a verb meaning "to work." Alex and his *droogs* (transliteration of the Russian word for friend or comrade) are contemptuous of any gainful employment other than burglary or "shop-crasting," and the word itself obviously suggests that one who "rabbits" must be something of a rabbit, habitually meek and scared. Rabbit is a modified form of the Russian verb *rabotat,* which means the same thing without the pejorative connotation, but we may reasonably conjecture that one of the reasons for its adoption into nadsat is its relation to the word *rab,* meaning "slave," as well as the English/Czech word *robot,* meaning "mechanical slave." The law compels all able-bodied adults, male and female, to work, but Alex and his friends consider one who does so to be as spiritless as a robot.

Implements of street warfare, such as bicycle chains, knives, and straight razors, bear their unaltered Russian names, which seem much more suggestive of the objects themselves than their English equivalent. A bicycle chain, for instance, its shiny coils shaken out along a sidewalk or whizzing through the night air, is so much more like an "oozy" than a "chain." There is something much more murderous about a "cutthroat britva" than a "cutthroat razor." This increased suggestiveness can also be seen in the loan names for parts of the human body. The primary social function of the tongue is strongly implied in the word *yahzick*, although not in the English equivalent. An orifice full of decaying "zoobies" is indeed more like a "rot" than a "mouth." The term *glazzies* is so much more suggestive than "eyes." A reader with a modicum of sensitivity can see that Burgess has not merely transliterated at random a lot of Russian words. He has carefully chosen words that are immensely more evocative to an English or American ear than their English equivalents, and he has, as I have said, modified some of them very plausibly. The word *grood*, for instance, might reasonably be expected to become "groody," even as one of its mildly vulgar English equivalents becomes "titty."

A good many of the non-Russian words in nadsat are derived from British slang. For example, a member of the city's finest, the ineffectual safeguard of law and order, is referred to as a "rozz." Although the word may be related to *rozha*, a colloquial expression roughly equivalent to "ugly mug," its direct ancestor is the English slang term *rozzer*, meaning "policeman." Tracing the origins of the nadsat vocabulary is an absorbing exercise for anyone with a feeling for language. The American edition of the novel has a glossary, prepared without any consultation with Burgess, which is not entirely accurate either in its translation of nadsat words or in the information it gives concerning their origins. The word *yarbles*, for instance, is glossed as a non-Russian word meaning "testicles." Indeed, it is used by Alex and his friends to designate the street fighter's favorite target of opportunity, but it is derived from the Russian word for apples (sing. *yabloko*). The Russian word itself occurs virtually unchanged in Alex's irreverent greeting to a high-ranking government official: "'Yarbles,' I said, like snarling like a doggie, 'Bolshy great yarblockos to thee and thine.'" Actually, after a few pages of the novel, a reader of even moderate sensitivity should not need a glossary, and he will do well to refrain from consulting this one, whose translations, even when they are accurate, may anchor him to terms that lack the rich onomatopoeic suggestiveness of Burgess's language. The following passage, for instance, in which Alex describes the orgiastic pleasure he derives from a violin concerto, would lose everything in translation:

As I slooshied, my glazzies tight shut to shut in the bliss that was better than any synthemesc Bog or God, I knew such lovely pictures. There were vecks and ptitsas, both young and starry, lying on the ground screaming for mercy, and I was smecking all over my rot and grinding my boot in their litsos. And there were devotchkas ripped and creeching against walls and I plunging like a shlaga into them, and indeed when the music, which was one movement only, rose to the top of its big highest tower, then, lying there on my bed with glazzies tight shut and rookers behind my gulliver, I broke and spattered and cried aaaaaaah with the bliss of it. And so the lovely music glided to its glowing close.

The novel is much more than a linguistic tour de force. It is also one of the most devastating pieces of multipronged social satire in recent fiction, and, like *The Wanting Seed,* it passes the test of "relevance." Although most people have been made aware of the assumptions of behavioral psychology through the recent uproar caused by Skinner's polemical restatement of his ideas in *Beyond Freedom and Dignity,* it is perhaps less generally realized that Skinner's schemes for imposing goodness on the human "mechanism" are among the less radical of those being proposed by behavioral technologists. As of this writing, a sociologist, Professor Gerald Smith of the University of Utah, is engaged in promoting the development of a device that can be implanted within the person of a paroled convict. The device, which measures adrenalin, is designed to send signals to a receiver in the home or office of his parole officer if the convict becomes excited by committing a crime. How this gadget would separate criminal stimuli from activities such as lovemaking that might signal "false positives" has not been revealed. What is certain, at least in the mind of the sociologist, is that the beneficial effects of such devices would completely justify their use. A convict would lose nothing, since, as a prisoner, he is already without freedom, and the benefits to society would be incalculable.

It is this line of thinking that Burgess challenges in *A Clockwork Orange.* He had been reading accounts of conditioning in American prisons, and it happened that as the teddy boys were being replaced on the streets by the mods and rockers, and youth was continuing to express its disdain for the modern state, a British politician put forward very seriously a proposal that obstreperous British youth should be conditioned to be good. At this point, Burgess says, "I began to see red and felt that I had to write a book." His protagonist Alex is one of the most appallingly vicious creations in recent fiction. Although his name was chosen because it suggested his composite Russian/English identity, it is ambiguous in other ways as well. The fusion of the negative prefix *a* with the word *lex* suggests simultaneously an absence of law and a lack of words. The idea of lawlessness is readily apparent in what we see of Alex's behavior, but the idea of wordlessness is subtler and harder to grasp, for Alex seems to have a great many words at his command, whether he happens to be snarling at his droogs in nadsat or respectfully addressing his elders in Russianless English. He is articulate but "wordless" in that he apprehends life directly, without the mediation of words. Unlike the characters who seek to control him and the rest of the society, he makes no attempt to explain or justify his actions in terms of abstract ideals or goals such as "liberty" or "stability." Nor does he attempt to define any sort of role for himself within a large social process. Instead, he simply experiences life directly, sensuously, and, while he is free, joyously. Indeed, his guiltless joy in violence of every kind, from the simple destruction or theft of objects to practically every form of sexual and nonsexual assault, is such that the incongruous term *innocent* is liable to come to a reader's mind.

Alex also has a fine ear for European classical music, especially Beethoven and Mozart, and although such widely differing tastes within one savage youngster seem incongruous, they are in fact complementary. Knowing his own passions, Alex is highly amused by the idea that great music is any sort of "civilizing" influence:

> I had to have a smeck, though, thinking of what I'd viddied once in one of these like articles on Modern Youth, about how Modern Youth would be better off if A Lively Appreciation Of The Arts could be like encouraged. Great Music, it said, and Great Poetry would like quieten Modern Youth down and make Modern Youth more Civilized. Civilized my syphilised yarbles. Music always sort of sharpened me up, O my brothers, and made me feel like old Bog himself, ready to make with the old donner and blitzen and have vecks and ptitsas creeching away in my ha ha power.

The first third of the novel is taken up with Alex's joyful satiation of all his appetites, and as rape and murder follow assault, robbery, and vandalism, we are overwhelmed by the spectacle of pleasure in violence. Although it might be argued that such psychopathic delight could not be experienced by a sane person, there is no implication in the novel that Alex is anything but sane—sane and free to choose what delights him. Since his choices are invariably destructive or harmful, it appears that society's right to deprive him of his freedom, if not his life, could hardly be disputed. What the novel does dispute is society's right to make Alex something less than a human being by depriving him of the very ability to choose a harmful course of action.

Partly as a result of his own vicious activities and partly as a result of struggles between Pelagian and Augustinian factions in government, Alex is destined to experience life as a well-conditioned "good citizen." The labels "Pelagian" and "Augustinian" are not used, but it is not very difficult to recognize these factions by their policies. The Pelagian-controlled government that is in power as the novel opens is responsible by its very laxness for the enormous amount of crime that occurs. When Alex is finally caught (while attempting to escape from a burglary involving a fatal assault on an old woman) it is mainly because his gang has betrayed him and facilitated the capture. He is sentenced to fourteen years in prison, and it is here that he will feel the effects of a major change in government policy.

The failure of liberal methods of government generates the usual DISAPPOINTMENT and the concomitant yearning for "Augustinian" alternatives. Realizing that the terrorized electorate cares little about "the tradition of liberty" and is in fact quite willing to "sell liberty for a quieter life," the government seeks to impose order by the most efficient means available. Unlike the Augustinian-controlled government in *The Wanting Seed*, this body does not resort to mass murder. Instead, it relies upon the genius of modern behavioral technology, specifically the branch of it that aims at the total control of human will. Alex, who brings attention to himself by murdering a fellow inmate, is selected as a "trailblazer" to be "transformed out of all recognition."

The purpose of Alex's transformation is to eliminate his capacity to choose socially deleterious courses of action. Psychological engineers force upon him what Professor Skinner might call "the inclination to behave." Strapped in a chair, he is forced to watch films of incredible brutality, some of them contrived and others actual documentaries of Japanese and Nazi atrocities during World War II. In the past violence has given him only the most pleasurable sensations; now he is suddenly overcome by the most unbearable nausea and headaches. After suffering a number of these agonizing sessions, he finds that the nausea has been induced not by the films but by injections given beforehand. Thus his body is being taught to associate the sight or even the thought of violence with unpleasant sensations. His responses and, as it were, his moral progress are measured by electronic devices wired to his body. Quite by accident, it happens that his body is conditioned to associate not only violence but his beloved classical music with nausea. The last movement of Beethoven's Fifth Symphony accompanies a documentary of the Nazis and the connection of the two with bodily misery is thus firmly fixed.

Finally, when his rehabilitation is complete, he is exhibited in all his "goodness" before an audience of government and prison officials. What is demonstrated on this occasion beyond all argument is that his body will not permit his mind to entertain even the thought of violence. When a hired actor insults and beats him, Alex must force himself to respond in a truly "Christian" manner, not only doing but willing good for evil. In a desperate effort to ease his misery, he literally licks the man's boots. This ultimate expression of submission will become, incidentally, one of the most memorable scenes in the Kubrick film. If one were seeking an illustration to place above a Skinnerian caption, such as "The Inclination to Behave" or "Operant Conditioning" or "Beyond Freedom and Dignity," one could hardly find one more vivid and arresting than the picture of Malcolm McDowell in the role of Alex licking the sole of the actor/antagonist's shoe.

A further demonstration proves that Alex is above sexual violence as well. When a ravishing, thinly clad young morsel approaches him on the stage, he is filled momentarily with an old yearning "to have her right down there on the floor with the old in-out real savage," but again his visceral "conscience" prevents him and he is able to stop the nausea only by assuming an almost Dantesque attitude of noncarnal adoration. Having thus gratified his rehabilitation engineers with proof that he is a "true Christian," Alex is free to enter society again — if not as a useful citizen, at least as a harmless one, and as living proof that the government is doing something to remedy social ills and thus merits reelection.

Alex is not only harmless but helpless as well, and shortly after his release he is the victim of a ludicrous, vengeful beating by one of his most helpless former victims, an old man assisted by some of his ancient cronies. Unable to endure even the violent feeling needed to fight his way clear, he is rescued by three policemen. The fact that one of his rescuers is a former member of his own gang and another a former leader of a rival gang suggests that the society is experiencing a transitional "Interphase" as it progresses into its Augustinian phase. These young thugs, like the "greyboys" in *The Wanting Seed,* have been recruited into the police force apparently on the theory that their criminal desires can be expressed usefully in the maintenance of order on the streets.

Again, we are tempted to suppose that Burgess was influenced by conditions in some American cities where, as he has remarked, the police

seem to represent little more than "a kind of *alternative* criminal body."
To some extent, he may have been influenced by such conditions, but the
political phenomena of which these hoodlum police are a symptom could
be observed in practically any society passing into a phase of Augustinian
reaction. The government accepts as axiomatic that order must be *imposed*
and that its imposition will probably require some form of violent force.
It is actually far less interested in suppressing crime than in simply maintaining stability and the appearance of order. Few citizens will question
the use of a hoodlum police force unless they happen to be its victims,
and those few include citizens whose opinions count for less than nothing
with an Augustinian government, since they are, for the most part, advocates of Pelagian alternatives. One of the marks of Augustinian government
is its total intolerance of political opposition. In this connection, we hear a
very significant remark by the minister of the interior at the time Alex is
selected for conditioning: "Soon we may be needing all our prison space
for political offenders." Again, as in *The Wanting Seed*, here, too, we are
reminded how Augustinianism may become fascism. We are reminded of
Nazi Germany where most of the imprisoned were political offenders, and
where common criminals in SS uniforms were the guardians of order.

Not surprisingly, Alex's former associates find his new situation
ideal for settling some old scores. They drive him down a lonely country
road and administer more than "a malenky bit of summary" with their
fists. Then, in a battered and even more helpless condition, he is left to
drag himself through pouring rain toward a little isolated cottage with
the name HOME on its gate. This little cottage happens to have been the
scene of one of the most savage atrocities he and his droogs had carried
out before his imprisonment, and one of the victims, a writer named F.
Alexander, is still living in it. F. Alexander had been beaten up by Alex
and his gang and forced to watch the four of them rape his wife, who had
died as a result. The writer has remained in the cottage devoting all his
energies to combatting the evils of "the modern age." Rightfully blaming
government failure as much as teenage savagery for his wife's death, he
seeks to discredit the government sufficiently to have it turned out of office in the next election.

F. Alexander's political and philosophical ideals incline toward
Pelagian liberalism and he has remained, in spite of his experience as a
victim of human depravity, committed to the belief that man is "a
creature of growth and capable of sweetness." Because of this, he remains
unalterably opposed to the use of "debilitating and will-sapping techniques of conditioning" in criminal reform. To some extent, he is an

autobiographical creation. Like Burgess, he has written a book entitled *A Clockwork Orange* with the purpose of illuminating the dangers of allowing such methods. The fact that he has had the sincerity of his beliefs about criminal reform tested by the personal experience of senseless criminal brutality is something else he shares with Burgess. We recall that during the war, while Burgess was stationed in Gibraltar, his pregnant wife was assaulted on a London street by American deserters and suffered a miscarriage as a result. But here the resemblance ends. Although Burgess believes man is capable of sweetness and should not be turned into a piece of clockwork, he is no Pelagian and his book, unlike F. Alexander's, is no lyrical effusion of revolutionary idealism ("written in a very bezoomy like style, full of Ah and Oh and that cal"). Most important, Burgess, unlike F. Alexander, is not blinded to concrete human realities by his political and philosophical ideals.

Since Alex and his droogs had been masked during their assault on HOME, F. Alexander does not recognize him. Filled with indignation against the state, he sees only another "victim of the modern age" who is in need of compassion. It soon occurs to him, however, that Alex can be used effectively as a propaganda device to embarrass the government — an example of the dehumanizing effects of its crime-control methods. He calls in three associates who share his beliefs and his enthusiasm for this idea. Although F. Alexander and his friends seem motivated by the loftiest of liberal ideas, it soon becomes apparent that they are incapable of seeing Alex as anything but a propaganda device. Like Swift's "projectors," they are so full of the abstract and the visionary that they have little concern for the suffering or welfare of individual human beings. To them Alex is not an unfortunate human being to be assisted but "A martyr to the cause of Liberty" who can serve "the Future and our Cause." When Alex asks F. Alexander to explain how he, as a will-sapped victim of the government, will benefit by being used as a propaganda device, the man is confused and unable to answer:

> He looked at me, brothers, as if he hadn't thought of that before and, anyway, it didn't matter compared with Liberty and all that cal, and he had a look of surprise at me saying what I said, as though I was being like selfish in wanting something for myself. Then he said: "Oh, as I say, you're a living witness, poor boy. Eat up all your breakfast and then come and see what I've written, for it's going into *The Weekly Trumpet* under your name, you unfortunate victim."

Although he is in no position to object, Alex realizes he is being treated "like a thing that's got to be just used" and is bitterly resentful.

In his anger, Alex lapses from polite, respectful English into snarling nadsat, a slip that, along with a few others, causes F. Alexander to remember the night his home was invaded. Although he cannot be certain Alex was one of the attackers, his suspicions begin to grow, and it is apparently because of this that a change is made in the plan for using Alex. The revolutionaries had originally planned to exhibit Alex at public meetings to inflame the people, but now they decide to make him a real martyr to their cause. Lest the people not be sufficiently shocked by the destruction of Alex's moral nature, they decide to have him destroyed completely by the government. As a dead "witness," he will be even more damning than a "living" one. They lock him in a flat and fill it with sounds of a loud and violent symphony in the hope he will be driven to suicide. Since he had already been considering suicide, the plan is immediately successful and he dives out a window, severely although not fatally injuring himself.

Among other things, this episode effectively underlines what Pelagian idealism shares with Augustinian cynicism. The Pelagian preoccupation with the tradition of liberty and the dignity of man, like the Augustinian preoccupation with stability, will make any sacrifice for the good of man worthwhile, including the destruction of man himself. But of course the revolutionaries do not view Alex as "man"; he is merely a human being who counts, as he himself perceives, for nothing more than a means to implement in a small way the great Pelagian scheme for the future. This ill-defined yet glorious dream, which causes these revolutionaries to use in such a fiendish and cynical manner the responses implanted in Alex by the Augustinian psychologists, might be equated in some respects with "The Idea" inspiring the revolutionaries in Dostoyevski's *The Possessed*. Dostoyevski's revolutionaries are of course nihilists, not Pelagians, but Burgess's implication seems to be that Pelagian revolutionary fervor is not far removed from nihilism. There is underlying both forms of enthusiasm a shared assumption that once the government is overthrown and corrupt institutions are destroyed, "man" will be saved. If individual men are obstacles to the salvation of man on earth, so much the worse for them. If they can be used as means to achieve the end, so much the better for the cause.

The Pelagian scheme very nearly succeeds, and while Alex is recovering in a hospital from his death dive, a power struggle rages. The government receives ample amounts of embarrassing publicity concerning the attempted suicide, but somehow survives. One day Alex awakens to find himself fully as vicious as before his treatment. More psychological engineers, using "deep hypnopaedia or some such slovo," have restored his moral nature, his "self," and his concomitant appetites for Beethoven and throat cutting. As he listens to the "glorious Ninth of Ludwig van," he exults,

> Oh, it was gorgeosity and yumyumyum. When it came to the Scherzo I could viddy myself very clear running and running on like very mysterious nogas, carving the whole litso of the creeching world with my cut-throat britva. And there was the slow and the lovely last singing movement still to come. I was cured all right.

The Augustinians are delighted. In this "depraved" condition, he cannot embarrass them further.

At this point, the American edition of *A Clockwork Orange* ends, and Stanley Kubrick, following the American edition very closely, ends his film. In its earlier British editions, however, the novel has one additional chapter that makes a considerable difference in how one may interpret the book. This chapter, like the chapters that begin the novel's three main parts, opens with the question. "What's it going to be then, eh?" Indeed, this is the question the reader has been left to ponder. We have seen Alex's depraved "self" replaced by a well-behaved "not-self," which is then replaced by the old "self" when he is "cured." We are led to believe that, aside from imprisonment or hanging, these two conditions are the only possible alternatives for Alex. The omitted chapter, however, reveals yet another alternative. Alex and a new squad of droogs are sitting in his old hangout, the Korova Milkbar, drinking hallucinogenic "milk-plus mesto" and getting ready for the evening. This is exactly the way the novel began, but whereas the opening chapter is a prelude to violence, this one reveals Alex becoming weary of violence. He leaves his gang and wanders alone through the streets reflecting on the changes in his outlook. Although the behaviorial engineers have managed to restore his old vicious self, he is becoming sentimental and starting to yearn for something besides the pleasure of indulging himself in classical music and the "old ultra-violence." What it is, he does not know, but when he encounters a member of his old gang who has married and settled down to a completely harmless, law-abiding existence, he realizes that this is what he wants for himself. He wants to marry and have a son. He will try to teach his son what he knows of the world, but he doubts that his son will be able to profit from his mistakes:

And nor would he be able to sop his own son, brothers. And so it would itty on to like the end of the world, round and round and round, like some bolshy gigantic like cheeloveck, like old Bog Himself (by courtesy of Korova Milkbar) turning and turning and turning a vonny grahzny orange in his gigantic rookers.

Burgess's explanation for the omission of this chapter in the American version is as follows:

He [Kubrick] followed the American edition which, in a kind of reverse version of Gresham's Law, will drive out the British version. The American edition has 20 chapters while the British edition has 21, and in the 21st chapter we have a scene enacted two years later than the final scene of the film. Alex is getting tired of violence and he meets one of his old friends who appears in the film, and sees him with a young girl going off to a wine and cheese party to play word games. So Alex thinks it's about time he got a girl and thought of getting married and having a son of his own, and he envisages the circle going around, the Orange turning in the paws of God, the Orange of the world turning. My American publisher in 1962 said, "I recognize that you are British and hence tend to a more pragmatic or milk-and-water tradition than we Americans know. We are tougher than you and prepared to end on a tough and violent note." And I said: "Well, if this is one of the conditions for publishing the book, get on with it."

This explanation, from an interview published in *Penthouse* magazine, suggests that Burgess tends to agree with his publisher, at least with regard to the superiority of the truncated American version. Certainly the omission of that twenty-first chapter causes the book to end on a very "tough and violent note."

The recurrent question, "What's it going to be then, eh?" becomes more difficult to answer because the dilemma posed by the book is a true one, *tertium non datur*. Assuming that Alex remains as he is when he awakens "cured," the society has the choice of either permitting him to exist as he is until, presumably, he kills someone else and is again confined, or imposing "goodness" and thereby being guilty of a moral evil more enormous than any of Alex's crimes. For political (not moral) reasons, of course, the government in the novel first impales the society on one horn and then on the other. Yet, even from a strictly moral standpoint, the choice can be very difficult. Although the Judaeo-Christian ethic clearly dictates that society should be governed on the assumption that man is and should remain an autonomous, responsible moral agent, this is by no means the last word on the subject for a great many individuals who, rightfully, consider themselves ethically sensitive. If one tries to persuade, say, a utilitarian that diminishing a criminal's ability to choose by conditioning or implanting gadgets is invariably evil and never justifiable from a moral standpoint, one is likely to become involved in lengthy and ultimately inconclusive debate. Utilitarian arguments in favor of achieving the greatest happiness for the greatest number by conditioning and, if you will, dehumanizing a few, can only be refuted if the Kantian principle that a person must be treated according to "the concept of a human being" and an end in himself, never a means, is accepted. Alex is no rule deontologist, but he objects to being used "like a thing that's like got to be just used." His outburst effectively illuminates the real question underlying the whole debate over conditioning: can it *ever* be right to use any human being as a nonhuman means to achieve an end, however noble or beneficient that end may be?

If the answer is "yes," we had better listen to Professor Skinner, for he and his behaviorist colleagues are seeking to provide the most effective and humane methods of using "man the mechanism" as a means of achieving the end of a stable culture. Although Skinner insists the culture he would design would be for "man," he also admits that man must be redesigned to fit this culture. He states explicitly in *Beyond Freedom and Dignity* that the culture he would design is "not for man as he is now" but for man as he may become under the benevolent shaping hand of science. If we are a bit chilled by this and change our answer to "ideally no but perhaps yes under extreme circumstances"—for example, a state of lawless chaos on the streets—we had still better listen to Professor Skinner, for once a society knowingly permits the dehumanizing use of one human being to achieve an end, it has effectively set in motion a process that must eventually involve all of its members. This is the warning Burgess gives us in *A Clockwork Orange,* and he gives it again in his essay *Clockwork Marmalade,* written shortly after he viewed the Kubrick film:

> Hitler was, unfortunately, a human being, and if we could have countenanced the conditioning of one human being we would have to accept it for all. Hitler was a great nuisance, but history has known others disruptive enough to make the state's

fingers itch—Christ, Luther, Bruno, even D. H. Lawrence.
One has to be genuinely philosophical about this, however
much one has suffered. I don't know how much free will man
really possesses (Wagner's Hans Sachs said: *Wir sind ein wenig
frei*—"we are a little free") but I do know that what little he
seems to have is too precious to encroach on, however good the
intentions of the encroachers may be.

This essay contains some very revealing explanations that should
help a great deal to clarify the meaning of Burgess's book and Kubrick's
film for those who misunderstood their parable as little more than a
glorification of violence. Burgess explains the novel's arresting title as
follows:

In 1945, back from the army, I heard an 80-year-old Cockney
in a London pub say that somebody was "as queer as a clockwork orange." The "queer" did not mean homosexual: it
meant mad. The phrase intrigued me with its unlikely fusion
of demotic and surrealistic. For nearly twenty years I wanted to
use it as the title of something. During those twenty years I
heard it several times more—in Underground stations, in
pubs, in television plays—but always from aged Cockneys,
never from the young. It was a traditional trope, and it asked
to entitle a work which combined a concern with tradition and
a bizarre technique. The opportunity to use it came when I
conceived the notion of writing a novel about brainwashing.
Joyce's Stephen Dedalus [in *Ulysses*] refers to the world as an
"oblate orange"; man is a microcosm or little world; he is a
growth as organic as a fruit, capable of colour, fragrance and
sweetness; to meddle with him, condition him, is to turn him
into a mechanical creation.

I quote this passage in full because it explains a good deal more than the
title. It also explains the inclusion of that rather optimistic last chapter in
the original British version. Again, Burgess is no Pelagian. Like most of
his more perceptive characters, he "accept[s] the myth of the Garden of
Eden and the Fall of Man." But if he has an Augustinian view of man as a
fallen creature, he also has a great deal of non-Augustinian hope for him
as a creature of growth and potential goodness. The message of the
chapter that was omitted is that, if there is hope, it is in the capacity of individuals to grow and learn by suffering and error. Suffering, fallen

human beings, not behavioral technology or the revolutionary schemes of idealists, bring "goodness" into the world. Awaiting this development is of course far less efficient or satisfying to some than imposing a design that ensures "goodness," but there is reason to hope that the wait will be worthwhile. Burgess is far more optimistic than Skinner, who has obviously lost all faith in man as he is and as he may become without the imposition of goodness.

In this same connection, Burgess continues his essay:

> Viewers of the film have been disturbed by the fact that Alex, despite his viciousness, is quite likeable. It has required a deliberate self-administered act of aversion therapy on the part of some to dislike him, and to let righteous indignation get in the way of human charity. The point is that, if we are going to love mankind, we will have to love Alex as a not unrepresentative member of it. The place where Alex and his mirror-image F. Alexander are most guilty of hate and violence is called HOME, and it is here, we are told, that charity ought to begin. But towards that mechanism, the state, which, first, is concerned with self-perpetuation and, second, is happiest when human beings are predictable and controllable, we have no duty at all, certainly no duty of charity.

He concludes with a note on the language, which, he says

> is no mere decoration, nor is it a sinister indication of the subliminal power that a Communist super-state may already be exerting on the young. It was meant to turn *A Clockwork Orange* into, among other things, a brainwashing primer. You read the book or see the film, and at the end you should find yourself in possession of a minimal Russian vocabulary—without effort, with surprise. This is the way brainwashing works. I chose Russian words because they blend better into English than those of French or even German (which is already a kind of English, not exotic enough). But the lesson of the *Orange* has nothing to do with the ideology or repressive techniques of Soviet Russia: it is wholly concerned with what can happen to any of us in the West, if we do not keep on our guard. If *Orange*, like *1984*, takes its place as one of those salutary literary warnings—or cinematic warnings—against flabbiness, sloppy thinking and overmuch trust in the state, then I will have done something of value.

That he has given us something of value cannot be disputed. Whether or not we choose to agree with the book as "a sermon on the power of choice," we have been forced to view clearly the implications of limiting that power. It is providential that the Kubrick film should come out in the same year as the publication of *Beyond Freedom and Dignity*. For those who were disturbed by Skinner's book but unable to articulate a refutation, Burgess and Kubrick have provided an eloquent answer.

BURGESS'S POSITION

Pelagius and Augustine appear in several of Burgess's other novels, and his treatment of their endless debate is consistent. Clearly, he views philosophical extremes — Pelagian, Augustinian, or whatever — as avenues to moral blindness and collective insanity, but any tendency to promote a generalized view of human nature is also liable to be a butt of his merciless satire. His satiric implication seems to be that both Pelagius and Augustine, as well as many of their philosophical heirs, have been hopelessly myopic in their analyses of the human condition. Their views of man have been determined and severely limited by preconceived notions about "man" that leave little room for the uniqueness of individual men. True, many of Burgess's most sympathetically drawn protagonists, such as Victor Crabbe in the *Malayan Trilogy*, Richard Ennis in *A Vision of Battlements,* and Mr. Woolton in *The Worm and the Ring,* are liberals, but they are totally ineffectual human beings. They are believers in social progress through the liberation of beneficent human energies, but they themselves can accomplish nothing, largely because they fail to understand the human beings around them. In fact, Burgess's most appealing characterizations, Hillier in *Tremor of Intent* and the Shakespeare/ Burgess composite hero in *Nothing Like the Sun,* actually lean toward Hobbist/Augustinian pessimism. The latter's pessimism may be due in part to the syphilis he catches from the Dark Lady, although he would not, in any case, accept the naïve Pelagianism of Southampton and the other supporters of Essex who seek to accelerate social progress through revolution. Most of his Hobbist/Augustinians, though, such as Dr. Gardner in *The Worm and the Ring* and Theodorescu in *Tremor of Intent,* are thoroughly repellant. They have a Hobbesian contempt for humanity and cynically assume that all power may and indeed should be gained by the manipulator who fully understands human weakness and malleability.

Pelagianism and detheologized Augustinianism actually share a great deal, as Burgess suggests in his first novel, *A Vision of Battlements*. We hear an American army officer describing how the Pelagian denial of original sin had spawned "the two big modern heresies — material progress as a sacred goal; the State as God Almighty." The former has produced "Americanism" and the latter, "the Socialist process." The officer points out that not only do the two heresies derive from the same ultimate source, they have also had essentially the same long-range consequences: "supra-regional goods — the icebox and the Chevrolet or the worker, standardized into an overalled abstraction at a standardized production belt." In other words, by exalting human potentiality and discarding Divine Grace, Pelagius and his heirs have actually reduced individual human signficances immeasurably. For when Divine Grace has no place, when sin in the Augustinian sense doesn't exist, when man is in need of nothing but a greater exertion of his will to improve his moral and spiritual condition, the only significant distributors of "grace" in any sense are the managers of the earthly communities wherein the effort must be made. It is these managers — corporation heads, "projecting" social scientists, commissars, bureaucrats, and others — who are most desirous of standardizing humanity, of bringing its affairs within the compass of their finite wisdoms. When Pelagianism really gains the upper hand, dominating the self-images of whole societies, civilization itself is threatened. This is what Mr. Enderby tries to convey in his long allegorical poem about the Minotaur, and in *The Worm and the Ring*, we hear Christopher Howarth suggesting the same thing in a drunken conversation with an American. For Howarth, America is a kind of clean-limbed, odorless, football-playing Theseus, and the Minotaur is original sin. The labyrinth is civilization itself. That this line of thinking is close to Burgess's own can be seen from his reflections on the Mei-lai massacre and the resultant national remorse. In his view, America had at last "discovered sin." It was, he seemed to feel, a not unhealthy discovery, for it is his belief that "a society that loses its sense of guilt is doomed."

Burgess's own leaning appears to be toward Augustinianism; yet he has clearly shown that the Augustinian tradition is just as inimical to the dignity of man, although it at least acknowledges a distinction between regenerate and unregenerate human nature. Since present-day Augustinian thinkers, like the Pelagians, have largely abandoned traditional orthodox Christian concepts of grace, the categories "regenerate" and "unregenerate" have meaning only with reference to social stability. One must subordinate one's "self" to the social machinery, become functionally or economically significant as a part of it, to be of the elect. The individual "self," asserting its existence by purely self-determined actions, is sand in the machinery of Augustinian society. In the detheologized Augustinian view, which is still very "Christian" in some respects, moral evil and self-assertion are so inextricably bound up with each other that they tend to be identified. As the murderous young hero of *A Clockwork Orange* tells us:

> More, badness is of the self, the one, the you or me on our oddy knockies, and that self is made by old Bog or God and is his great pride and radosity. But the not-self cannot have the bad, meaning they of the government and the judges and the schools cannot allow the bad because they cannot allow the self. And is not our modern history, my brothers, the story of brave malenky selves fighting these big machines? I am serious with you, brothers, over this. But what I do I do because I like to do.

"These big machines" are both Pelagian and Augustinian, and the contest between them, which manifests itself in the debates of intellectuals, and the actual "waltzing" of governments from blind conservatism to blind liberalism and back are symptomatic of Western man's acceptance of a faulty dilemma. Presumably, sanity and vision could lead men to a rejection of both "Pelagian" and detheologized "Augustinian" extremism and a recreation of society based upon realistic assessments of individual human potentiality. Without an increase of sanity and vision, Western man will become progressively dehumanized by Pelagian and Augustinian machines that seek to destroy the "self" to save "man." Eventually, he may be forced into the dilemmas Burgess has presented in these dystopian books. Once he, "man," is thus confined, it will not be up to the "malenky selves" to choose between the dehumanizing alternatives available.

TIMOTHY R. LUCAS

The Old Shelley Game:
Prometheus and Predestination
in Burgess's Works

Read The Ambassadors *and you can confidently say you have read Henry
James. But surely a profound theme needs tackling again and again?*
                              —ANTHONY BURGESS, *The Novel Now*

*Anyone reading Anthony Burgess' novels eventually asks himself, Haven't
I covered this ground before? The answer is invariably, Yes!*
                              —A. A. DEVITIS, *Anthony Burgess*

One of the most prolific English novelists of this century, Anthony
Burgess has managed (in the publication of forty-five books since 1956)
to sustain an almost inhumanly high level of quality in his writings.
Though Burgess has regularly, to his own vociferous displeasure, been
berated by critics for his self-confident fecundity, the haste of his transi-
tions from book to book has led to a revealing and, I believe, insufficiently
studied transparency in the borders of his fiction. These areas—wherein
the inspirations behind each novel visibly overlap, mutate, and stream
out in new paths of pursuit—are as worthy of our attention as the main
bodies of the books themselves; indeed, they constitute the very lifelines
of Burgess's art; they afford his readers bonus-like glimpses of the sources
which have stimulated him and, subsequently, his work, so that we are
granted not only works of have-at-you vigor and dazzling wit but, in

From *Modern Fiction Studies* 27, no. 3 (Autumn 1981). © 1981 by the Purdue Research
Foundation.

these clear and vital junctions, the stark evidence of Burgess's reading lists, his turns of thought, his historical supposings, his most central obsessions.

Geoffrey Aggeler, among others, has noted that the idea for *Nothing Like the Sun* can be seen "twitching itself to life well before the year of the Shakespeare quadricentennial" in the latter pages of *The Right to an Answer*, which precedes that No-Holds-Bard conjecture by several years. A long-lived captivation with Shakespeare's rival playwright, Christopher Marlowe, begun with Burgess's 1940 master's thesis at Manchester University, has had a wide influence on his published works, ranging from the perfectly appropriate (the mentions in *English Literature*, *Shakespeare*, and *Nothing Like the Sun*) to the quakingly gratuitous (King Herod's murmur of "Knifed in a tavern brawl" in *Man of Nazareth*) to the Joyceanly neo-mythic (Hillier's evolution from spy to saint in *Tremor of Intent* dramatizes to some extent Burgess's personal feelings about Marlowe, as expressed in *Shakespeare* and in the essay "Dr. Rowstus") to the inspirationally misplaced (Keats's cursing death in *Abba Abba*). In his *Paris Review* interview, Burgess traced the origins of yet another recurring theme, that of the relationship between genius and disease (a motif which colors the Shakespeare novel, as well as *Inside Mr. Enderby* and *Abba Abba*), back to Mann's *Doctor Faustus* and personal experience.

> I became interested in syphilis when I worked for a time in a mental hospital full of GPI cases. I discovered there was a correlation between the spirochete and mad talent. The tubercle also produces a lyrical drive. Keats had both. Oh, you'll want examples of these GPI talents. There was one man who'd turned himself into a kind of Scriabin, another who could give you the day of the week for any date in history, another who wrote poems like Christopher Smart. Many patients were orators or grandiose liars. It was like being imprisoned in a history of European art.

Both *Abba Abba* and *1985*, as well, are traceable to the same paragraph in Burgess's *Shakespeare* biography, in which he writes:

> The octave rhymed on the pattern ABBA ABBA, so that there were only two rhymes—easy enough in Italian, where many words have identical endings, as with *amore, cuore, fiore, dolore,* but not so easy with English, which is short of rhymes.

The fact of this shortage, you will remember, sends a poet to Room 101 in Orwell's *Nineteen Eighty Four*: he can find only one suitable rhyme for "rod," and that once holy name is inadmissable in the superstate.

Given how early such predominant themes in later Burgess can be glimpsed in separate, embryonic context, these connections could be argued as being the implicit manifestation of predestination in his oeuvre. Burgess has written comically and truthfully and extensively — in *The Novel Now*, the essay "Genesis and Headache," and his Hemingway primer — about the physically debilitating aspect of novel writing, and of the agoraphobias associated with authorship, and has also published several fictional manifestos on the theme of threatened freedom of will; the latter is important to my argument for, as Burgess writes in his most recent novel, *Earthly Powers*: "To foreknow would be to abrogate that gift (from God — of utter freedom), for what can be foreseen is predestined, and where there is predestination there is no freedom of will." As Burgess writes with a mentally interred list of novels yet to write — *Saturday Review* recently pinned him down to "a Jane Austen novel in the form of a Mozart symphony," "a novel that's the history of the British state," "a long novel about life since 1945," and more — it could be said that he and the authors who share his situation have planned the majority of their remaining lives on paper, to the exclusion of personal freedom. Burgess's handiwork can help us to enjoy, defend, and preserve our personal freedoms, but to the relative restriction of his own (he is said to work eight hours a day, seven days a week). Rather like the Moses he reawakened in script and verse, his vocation somewhat forbids his stepping into the Promised Land.

Naturally any analysis of so widespread a phenomenon must, of necessity, be fairly limited in scope. I have selected *MF* for my primary focus because it acts as something of a watershed in the Burgess oeuvre. A successful and completely original experiment, *MF* is certainly the most concentrated prose of average novel-length Burgess has yet produced, and it was produced at a time of great upheaval and transition.

Burgess's first wife, Llewella Isherwood Jones (with whom he translated two French novels), died after a prolonged illness in March 1968, and, some months after, when Burgess remarried, he left England with new wife Liliana Macellari (and son Andreas) for a long spell of continental browsing. *MF,* which is sedulously based on the structuralist theories of Claude Lévi-Strauss, was the first novel Burgess wrote *in toto* in his second marriage's fresh surroundings. This novel initiates an unusually broad and long thematic thread, which endures in one form or another through *Man of Nazareth*: the foreign (typically English) man's plight in confronting the provocative and eternal strangeness that is Rome, a confrontation which produces such disparate results as new love and crucifixion amongst thieves.

The flavors, scents, and commotions of unfamiliar territory are remarkably pungent in the crackling language of *MF,* but the novel is not—despite its sexual crux—in many ways a sensual experience. In a review of *MF,* Ralph McInerny bemoaned that "One would feel a good deal happier about this novel if it did not seem so open an invitation to be made the subject of interpretative papers at *PMLA"* and that it was too much like "one of those literary quizzes which show up in the book sections of Sunday papers." Even Geoffrey Aggeler's book, a milestone in Burgess study, gives *MF* a kind of *caveat emptor,* warning that it "demands too much in the way of 'intellectual' involvement," while adding later that "just as strong-gutted and agile-witted playgoers can find *Troilus and Cressida* or *Measure for Measure* more rewarding than Shakespeare's early romances, so a reader can find *MF* more rewarding."

It seems absolutely natural that Burgess would be attracted to structuralism and its blendability with fiction, particularly if one appreciates how richly the works of Joyce and Shakespeare have affected his creations; indeed, without at least a single reading of *Ulysses* under his belt, the reader stands no chance of grasping the full nature of Burgess's motivational propulsions, whether they result in the nuances of Night-town in Dr. Edwin Spindrift's prowl through the English underbelly in *The Doctor Is Sick* or the poignant "deserves to live, deserves to live" which underscores *The Clockwork Testament*'s dedication to actor Burt Lancaster. Both Shakespeare and Joyce spent time in revitalizing the art of their elders, and Burgess spent much of his career prior to *MF* experimenting with this particular aspect of his masters' craft, unaware of the plan's alignment with what Lévi-Strauss's relatively new science has to say about our living in a duoverse and the sharing (between the two universes) of certain archetypes. "I'm interested in what structuralism can teach us about myth," Burgess told *The Paris Review*. "Existing myths carry useful depth, a profundity of meaning which saves the novelist from a lot of inventive trouble."

Burgess has obviously been actively testing the malleability of fiction and mythic appliance since his very first novel, *A Vision of Battlements,* written in 1949, in which his own wartime memories of Gibralter are adjusted to "facsimile" Virgil's *Aeneid*. In the novel's "Foreword," written for the novel's belated first publication in 1965, Burgess explains that "The use of an epic framework, diminished and made comic, was not mere pedantic wantonness, nor was it solely a little tribute to James Joyce; it was a tyro's method of giving his story a backbone." The next book written, *The Eve of St. Venus,* a 1950 work published in England in 1964 and in America in 1970, announces on its title page that "This is based on a tale told by Burton (*Anatomy of Melancholy:* Pt. 3, Sec. 2, Mem. 1, Subs. 1) which he got from Florilegus, ad annum 1058." Even so recent an endeavor as *Napoleon Symphony* finds Burgess, though well out of the "tyro" category, still dabbling in the fleshing of fiction on the bonetrack of some other art, in this case Beethoven's *Eroica* Symphony. In an essay entitled "The Good Companion," which reviews Sir Paul Harvey's *Oxford Companion to English Literature,* Burgess demonstrates how even innocuous, random facts may be converted "at a pinch" into an entertaining narrative:

> The point for me has been chiefly the fructifying value, on a practising writer sometimes desperate for ideas, of a casual browsing through any two facing pages. I open at random: pages 446 and 447. These take me from Kennedy, Margaret (author of *The Constant Nymph*) to Kierkegaard, Soren Aabye. Good, I shall write a novel about an Anglo-Dane called Soren Kennedy, who lives in Kensington and is doing research on St. Mungo (who is also St. Kentigern). Discovering that this saint probably sojourned for a time on the Isle of Man (Keys, House of), he goes to Douglas, where he meets a beautiful Arab divorcee called Khadijah.

Burgess is able to follow this structurally sound, albeit outrageous, plot for more than an additional (progressively fantastic) paragraph and draws the essay to a close with some advice for fellow writers:

> The *Companion* has 961 pages, so no writer, especially a novelist, need ever be short of material. At a pinch he can always refurbish a plot by Meredith, Scott, or Hardy. There is no end to the uses of Harvey, as I know. As I very well know. As I know as well as any literary man living.

Certain passages in *MF* are blatantly derived from the random pages of such factual guides as a world atlas (p. 41, in the Knopf, 1971 edition), an encyclopedia (pp. 75–76, 109), a baseball manual (p. 81), and a tourist guidebook (pp. 238–39). The encyclopedia extractions, in particular, remind one that Burgess must have been using this technique as far back as *One Hand Clapping,* to prepare questions for TV quiz shows. The result of such experimentation often takes the form of lengthy lists, rather reminiscent in themselves of those adorning the pages of *The Right to an Answer,* a stylistic ornamentation which Burgess has formally accredited to the influence of Nabokov and *Lolita.* But this, as I say, is the most obvious fruit of the procedure. There exist more subliminal uses for this approach, as Burgess details in this excerpt from a *Writer's Digest* interview:

> What I often do nowadays when I have to, say, describe a room, is to take a page of a dictionary, any page at all, and see if, with the words suggested by that one page, I can build up a room, build up a scene. This is the kind of puzzle that interests me, keeps me going, and it will even suggest how to describe a girl's hair, at least some of it will come, but I must keep to that page. I even did it in the novel I wrote called *MF.* There's a description of a hotel vestibule whose properties are derived from Page 167 in W. J. Wilkinson's *Malay English Dictionary.* Nobody has noticed this. The thing, you see, it suggests what pictures are on the wall, what color somebody's wearing, and, as most things in life are arbitrary anyway, you're not doing anything naughty — you're really doing what Nature normally does, you're just making an entity out of the elements.

Burgess has defended the cold-bloodedness apparent in this rather schematic literary exercise by citing the rigorous structural laws which govern the sonnet, which, if in the hands of a master, can obviously be used to convey great warmth and sympathy. What this approach also conveys is a curiously engaging sense of superstition that heightens the supernatural side of *MF's* foreshadowing technique, in which our hero Miles Faber's lawyer Loewe looks ahead to Llew (Faber's scatologically minded twin), as does Professor Keteki to Kitty Kee, the SCREW MAILER graffiti (p. 17) to the Mailer novel on Faber's assignated screw-mate Irma's rather manly bookshelf (p. 27), and the paperback novel *Faggots for the Burning* (p. 39) to the upcoming appearance of gay shipmates Chandeleur and Aspinwall (p. 54), *ad infinitum;* all this, in turn, enlarges *MF's* vista of crumbling free will, turning over the steering of Faber's fated adventure to predestining forces. Just as Miles Faber — whose name means "skilled worker" — is irresistibly pulled by the scherzo of this escalatingly coincidental vacuum, which will force him into the commission of incest with his sister Catherine, Burgess — who has frequently referred to himself as a "skilled craftsman" — restricts his own free choice of words to an arbitrarily chosen page of alphabetized (or incestuously catalogued and/or categorized) words and names. In other words, the means of composition steadily and suicidally erect the very sense of order that the forthcoming act of incest, according to Lévi-Strauss's teachings, is intended to collapse.

To move from form to content, it seems likely, to judge from *MF*'s frequent subliminal emphases of Percy Bysshe Shelley and his lyrical drama *Prometheus Unbound*, which I will survey momentarily, that Burgess (at some time concurrent with his move from disappointing Malta to holy Rome) took it upon himself to compare notes with other Rome-transplanted Englishmen of letters, before adding *MF* to the chain of their literature. It is interesting to note, in keeping with *MF*'s riddling nature and obsessive egg-*cum*-bird-*cum*-egg (which came first?) imagery, that Shelley first became entwined with both in *One Hand Clapping*. In the passage in question, Janet Shirley describes her husband Howard's appearance on a TV quiz program, where he intends to make use of a photographic memory, well steeped in encyclopedic reading, to win the jackpot:

> "Anyway," Laddie said, "which would be better for break-fast, Shakespeare or Bacon?"
> "That's a bloody silly question."
> The audience didn't know what to make of that, and I blushed because that was typical of Howard, but the quizmaster, that is to say Laddie, just laughed it off and said, "It's meant to be a silly question, because the first question always is." Then Howard turned on a big smile and said:
> "All right, Bacon, but I'd like something Shelley with it." Nobody in the audience saw that, but Laddie yelled his head off and said, "Very good, very good indeed, meaning, of course, that an egg is shelly. Excellent."

The next mention of Shelley significant to *MF* is to be found in the pages of the novel Burgess has last completed at the time of *MF*'s composition, *Enderby Outside:*

> When Shelley said what he said about poets being the un-acknowledged legislators of the world, he wasn't really using fancy language. It's only by the exact use of words that people understand themselves.

Of course, the pervasive guiding legend of the (ultimately apocryphal) poet Sib Legeru, whose supposedly illuminating works of "antiart" compel Faber to the isle of Castita and the consummation of his predestined fate, fulfills Shelley's observation by establishing most of the behavioral laws and familial connections between Faber and the novel's supporting characters. As Z. Fonanta reveals to an astonished Faber in chapter nineteen, "Sib Legeru" is actually a catch-all pseudonym ("It means legging or ligging or lying with one's own sib, it means *incest*" [p. 233]) whose works are a mixture of contributions from several members of the Faber colony; it thus reflects the family's incestuous reflex, as does Faber's mind-felt wish to emulate his master's style. Taken in this light, the secondary observation of the *Enderby Outside* quotation — that "It's only by the exact use of words that people understand themselves" — has the ring of prophetic, predestined criticism of Legeru's legacy of pseudo-art and Faber's own artistic ambitions which, as his idealized play sequence (p. 57) indicates, inclines toward the meaningless and insubstantial. The murkiness enshrouding Legeru's identity and meaning throughout the novel are indeed the obstacles Faber encounters in knowing himself, and the Legeru oeuvre is found in an abandoned shed *because* it reflects incestuous qualities which must be shed and abandoned.

But the real assertion of Shelley in *MF* is to be found in its debt to *Prometheus Unbound*. This was the first major work Shelley produced after settling in Rome, and thus mirrored Burgess's situation. This drama, written between 1818–1819 (somewhat concurrent with the writing of Mary Shelley's *Frankenstein, or the Modern Prometheus*), the play dramatized in lyric verse the ordeal of Prometheus, chained by Jupiter to a crag in the Indian Caucasus, where each day a vulture would descend to devour his perpetually regenerated liver, as recompense for his having stolen fire from the heavens to alleviate the miseries of mankind. Shelley replaces the vulture with a chorus of furies, mirrored in *MF* by a chorus of quizzing birds in the performing ensemble of Aderyn the Bird Queen, the mother of Llew — "I forget their names," Faber regrets, "let us say they were: Iris, Angus, Charles, Pamela, John, Penelope, Brigid, Anthony, Muriel, Mary, Norman, Saul, Philip, Ivy" (p. 110). Aderyn later uses the birds to taunt Faber, impersonating the accidentally-murdered Llew, with questions (riddles) designed to smoke him out (pp. 223–26). Aderyn's hawks are trained to attack his eyes at the first incorrect answer he gives, thus achieving a parallel not only with *Prometheus Unbound* (which would not have been reason enough), but with Sophocles' *Oedipus Rex*, whose relationship with *MF* is obvious and well chronicled elsewhere.

Judging from how many of the novel's narrative turns were arbitrarily decided from (predominantly) lexical sources, it is likely that Burgess's toying with Promethean symbolism was initiated on the primary level of the name's Greek lexical formation; it comes, says Webster, from the Greek *pro* (meaning "before") and *mathien* (to "learn" or "see"). The name means "foresight," which would imply a Promethean share in the responsibility for *MF*'s extensive foreshadowing technique. Other relevant forms of prometheus would be the *Callosamia promethea,* a large bombycid moth, and the promethean match, which preceded in general use the friction match of modern day; these symbols can combine to illustrate, within the very word "Prometheus," the fatal attraction of Moth to Flame and, metaphorically, Faber's fated attraction toward the solving of riddles and the poetry of Sib Legeru, which pull him ever nearer to the incestuous act he hopes to avoid.

Like Mary Shelley's Frankenstein, Miles Faber is a modern Prometheus. The resemblance, however, is more figurative (that is to say "comic") than actual (that is to say "mythic"). The fact that Faber is black, of which we aren't informed until the novel's final pages, is foremost an example of "false classifications" (Aggeler), but it also shows us, on this comic and figurative level, how chained Faber has been preconceptually to a prejudicial Caucasian crag. What seems to be a urine theme (see pp. 21, 40–42, 111) begins as an anthropological affectation, with an angry Faber using his "always strongly aromatic" urine "like a cat asserting its right through smell," but ultimately becomes, through Burgess's comic intentions, his parallel to Promethean liver-loss. Also, while the isle of Castita (Italian for "chastity") is certainly an infuriated parody of Malta — where Burgess found his mail regularly edited by censors — it may also be read as a contemporary and also figurative version of the Promethean isle of chastisement.

The only direct reference to *Prometheus Unbound* appears in *MF* on pp. 116–17 as Faber passes an establishment called "the Magus Emporium" (something of a bird symbol in itself, as it reminds us of John Fowles), when

> an uneasy recollection of Professor Keteki's lectures came up like the taste of an old meal. Shelley. Was it *Prometheus Unbound*? Llew the Fucking Free, nonsense. The lines were:
>
> *The Magus Zoroaster, my dead child, Met his own image walking in the garden. That apparition, sole of men, he saw. For know there are two worlds of life and death —*

What came after? And why did he meet his own image? I
couldn't remember. Not that it mattered much.

In the latter part of this excerpt, Burgess establishes a riddle that will go
unanswered, except subliminally, unless the reader seeks knowledge outside the incestuous bounds of his novel, while underplaying the importance of the allusion with a "Not that it mattered much." But what *does*
come after? Why did Zoroaster meet his own image, and what
transpired? What is Miles Faber so conveniently unable to recall to mind?
Shelley's poem continues:

> For know there are two worlds of life and death:
> One that which thou beholdest; but the other
> Is underneath the grave, where do inhabit
> The shadows of all forms that think and live
> Til Death unite them and they part no more.
>   (act 1, ll. 195–99)

The same sentiment, more or less, finds subliminal expression on a section of Chandeleur's slogan-riddled T-shirt: "*The fear of solitude is at
bottom the fear of the double, the figure which appears one day and
always heralds death,*" attributed, in Faber's annotating confusion, to
"St. Lawrence Nunquam" or "Cnut of Alexandria." Obviously, it is the
sentiment, then, of Lawrence Durrell, whose *Alexandria Quartet* was
Italianized by the "Liana" to whom *MF* and all of Burgess's subsequent
work is dedicated. Incidentally, there is much in Zoroastrianism befitting
MF's thematic intentions, notably the bearing of the religion's dualism
(between the "Wise Lord" and Ahriman, the "Evil One") on the structuralist view that ours is not a universe, but a duoverse, as well as the
religion's basis in original choice, which returns us to Burgess's central,
supernatural theme of Free Will, which is lost in Zoroastrianism once
original choice has been made when the dualism is replaced by an enduring monotheistic approach. The original purpose, then, for the inclusion
of the Shelley lines is to foreshow or forethink or prometheate Faber's
ultimate confrontation with Llew, which ends in the twin's death, which
does "unite them and they part no more," thereby locking Faber into an
impersonation that speeds him down the track toward his "marriage" to
sister Catherine. Pretty good results for a "Not that it mattered much."

   The fact that Burgess would (or Faber would) have us accept the *Prometheus* excerpt as a gratuitous doo-dad is reminiscent of his similarly
cavalier denial of *MF*'s Jam-Jellies-Jelyf-Jellif theme, which resembles a
verbal descent into Finneganese dreaminess and acknowledgedly rattles

around inside the novel like a loose screw. After a number of metamorphic mentions (ranging from the "Shakespeareanly" optical metaphor of *jellies* [p. 112] to *Jellif*, a brand of gelatin for which Catherine professes a dependent fondness [p. 138]), Faber confronts Z. Fonanta—who comes forth as Faber's grandfather—with the substance, demanding to know its relevance. Fonanta's reply is evasive, but encouraging:

> I once suggested the name [Jellif] to a marketing firm in New York. May I say how glad I am to see you looking for connections, tightening bolts that aren't there, soldiering on despite your manifest weariness, hammering away at structures.
>
> (p. 232)

A few paragraphs later, there is a gleam from the "bolts that aren't there." Fonanta reveals that he was punished by the gods for his own act of incest, with his mother, when he was "run over by a tramcar in Lille." This should remind the hammering reader that, among the first clues in this thematic arc of preserves, there is a conversation between two of the "talkers" in Aderyn's troupe of performing birds:

> A falsetto mynah cried:
> —*Oh mummy dear what is that stuff that looks like strawberry jam?* A gruff starling responded:
> —*Hush hush my child it's only dad run over by a tram.*
>
> (p. 112)

Since Aderyn must have been the one to instruct the birds in this patch of sick verse, the "dad" appearing in the second line could be read as an implication of a familial tie between Fonanta and herself, which would cement Faber's brotherhood and twinship with the late, unlamented Llew. Fonanta goes so far as to admit that Faber's incestuously wrought family had once included "a brief supererogatory twin" but that Faber, his sister Catherine, and himself now "represent the total remnant of a once large and flourishing family" (p. 230). The admission, however, does not allow for Aderyn's survival following her blinding by her birds (chapter twenty briefly infers that she was able to continue her career as Aderyn the Blind Bird Queen [p. 242]), so the structure of the Jellif theme ultimately peters out into nothing. This still could be intentional, as it can be interpreted as a symbol of a mass-marketed preservation of the pure familial essence, an essence marketed to be consumed by the fruit of its "*own flesh, his own flesh.*" In other words, a view of incest as, to quote Miles Faber, "a kind of cannibalism" (p. 139). The degeneration of preserves to jelly to gelatin to Jellif illustrates the slow pollution of pure preserves with artificial preservatives, just as uninterrupted incest will eventually leave family lineage looking like xeroxes of xeroxes.

There remain certain stylistic comparisons to be drawn before *Prometheus Unbound* may be dismissed. In his preface to the poem, Shelley grants us a glimpse of the Rome in which it was written:

> This poem was chiefly written upon the mountainous ruins of the Baths of Caracalla, among the flowery glades, and thickets of odiferous blossoming trees, which are extended in ever widening labyrinths upon its immense platforms and dizzy arches suspended in the air. The bright blue sky of Rome, and the effect of the vigorous awakening spring in that divinest climate, and the new life with which it drenches the spirits even to intoxication, were the inspiration of this drama.

This detailed, enraptured reportage is strikingly alike in tone to *MF*'s science fictional chapter 20, in which an aged Faber observes with bittersweet notation a stormy Braccianese landscape in "the last summer of the second Christian millenium." This remarkable chapter actually mirrors much of Shelley, from his preface to *Prometheus Unbound*, to the final act of that play (in that both are written from vantages of afterthought and achieve the most overwhelming lyricism of their respective wholes), to the 1824 poem entitled "Song." Compare stanzas 5 and 6 of this poem to the final, exultant paragraph of *MF*:

> I love all that thou lovest,
>   Spirit of Delight!
> The fresh earth in new leaves dressed,
>   And the starry night;
> Autumn evening, and the morn
> When golden mists are born.
>
> I love the snow, and all the forms
>   Of the radiant frost;
> I love waves, and winds, and storms,
>   Everything almost
> Which is Nature's...

I enjoy the movement of life — kids falling in love, performing birds. . . . new *gelato* flavors, ceremonies, anthills, poetry, loins, lions, the music of the eight tuned Chinese pipes suspended from an economically carved and highly stylized owl head at our window facing the lake maddened into the sweetest cacophony by a *tramontana* that will not abate its passion, the woman calling her son in (his name is Orlando and she says his father will be *furioso*). . . . anything in fact that's unincestuous.

Considering that Julian Mitchell has described how the closing lines of *The Wanting Seed* are derived from Valery's "Le Cimetière marin," it would not be unusual for Burgess to conclude *MF* according to the structure and lilt of an ancestral, poetic plan. To be sure, Faber's sprawling list of the "unincestuous" artifacts which lend landscape to his advancing years are, more often than not, transparent touchstones of the incestuously woven work of art we have, with this final paragraph, finished reading. Faber may enjoy "new *gelato* flavors," but surely Jellif by any other name. . . .

The Promethean ingredients of *MF* would amount to no more than a finely detailed and isolated formula were they not carried over into other projects. But the fact that they were makes them even more important and influential.

Burgess's next novel, *Napoleon Symphony*, enlivens its third section (or "movement") of four with a stage presentation of a Prometheus play, presumably meant to emphasize: (1) Beethoven's own infusing of themes from this 1801 *Die Geschöpfe des Prometheus* ballet into the third movement of the *Eroica* Symphony, as a subliminal slap at Napoleon Bonaparte; (2) Napoleon's own "predestined" exile on the island of St. Helena; and (3) the sheer unproducibility not only of Shelley's drama but of Thomas Hardy's megascopic *The Dynasts*, which Burgess terms, in the novel's conclusive epistle, "a monstrous shocking failure." As the novel follows the charted scheme of Beethoven's symphonic score, Napoleon is more or less replaced by Prometheus from the Third Movement on, becoming, in the Fourth Movement, "basically Promethapoleon, chained to a rock, his liver eagled out."

The title of Beethoven's ballet (which translates as *The Creatures of Prometheus*), in addition to the presuggestion of Shelley's influence over *MF*, must have been the factors responsible for the *Frankenstein* motif which unravels in the novella *Beard's Roman Women*, in which Burgess's predestination theme is granted full supernatural shape as the theme of artistic imprisonment is brought comically to the fore.

In this book, the recently widowed screenwriter Ron Beard is summoned by Hollywood to prepare a screen musical based on the Swiss summer enjoyed by Lord Byron and the two Shelleys, during which Mary's book *Frankenstein* was written. Beard finds new, rejuvenating love in Hollywood and follows his objet d'amour, a photographer named Paola, back to Rome, where he sets about writing "*The Lovers of the Lake* (tentative title)." The predestining force is personified as Leonora, Beard's deceased first wife, who contacts him not only by telephone, but on a few subliminal levels (for example, she appears on a taxi radio in the form of the musical group The Grateful Dead); this, of course, makes Mary Shelley's theme of reanimated corpses, in this referential context, more dimensional and, therefore, more than ornamental. As for the theme of artistic imprisonment, Beard is attacked in the apartment he shares with Paola (she is off on assignment) by four Italian girls bent on demonstrating the expanse of their sexual liberation and, in a surprising parody of the rape scene in *A Clockwork Orange,* is stripped, ridiculed, forced to watch his love nest defiled, and left without clothes (seen as the mode of escape) in a wrecked room with only his script and typewriter to keep him sane. The *Clockwork* rape was, as Burgess has recounted in numerous articles and interviews, used as a means to exorcise memories of the attack his first wife suffered, at the hands of American war deserters, in 1943. Remembering that this attack led to complications which resulted in her death twenty-five years later, one can see the importance of reactivating and updating the old scene to illustrate a sense of abandonment, and of shedding a meaningful glow on life's only constant.

Beard's Roman Women concludes with Beard remarried to Ceredwin, apparently the sister of his first wife, and they playfully converse as *Milford Lucifer* (the release title of the *Frankenstein* project) unreels on television:

> "Funny thing, incest. Nothing to do with blood, really. Mystical you could call it. *He copulated with his late wife's sister.* That sounds terrible, doesn't it?"
>
> "*She copulated with her dead sister's husband.* That sounds worse. I can see how it might turn somebody on, somebody a bit, you know, unbalanced."

There is certainly nothing unbalanced about the permutations these themes have made in their passages from book to book, as they hearby come full circle, back to *MF* territory, and return on a resounding note of renewal.

Although it isn't the only such instance of book-to-book communication, this Promethean matrix may well be the major one and stands as a prime, if not too obvious, example of one of Anthony Burgess's most personal accomplishments as an author. Not only has he given us an extraordinary body of imaginative fiction: he has veined that body with an equally extraordinary system of circulatory intents.

GEOFFREY AGGELER

Faust in the Labyrinth:
Earthly Powers

It seems hardly coincidental that the most significant attempts in postwar western fiction to explain twentieth-century history are novels with Faustian protagonists. Unquestionably the greatest of these is Thomas Mann's *Doctor Faustus*, in which, through the characterization of Adrian Leverkühn and his friend Zeitblom, we are made to see how all of the impulses and ideals which had produced the greatness of German culture were inextricably bound up with the forces which had produced Nazism. Very nearly on the same level of achievement and equally large in scope is Malcolm Lowry's *Under the Volcano*, mirroring in its drunken protagonist the world itself on the brink of war in 1938. Both of these novels embrace within their depictions of the Faustian quest the forces which had but recently threatened and were still to some extent threatening the very survival of western civilization. To an extent, both of them reflect Spengler's thesis that the spirit of modern Europe and America is Faustian, that civilized western man is aging and wasted, effete, infirm, and defenseless, yet still hopeful of achieving everything, including the impossible. But both novelists, influenced by events Spengler did not live to see, go well beyond him in emphasizing the vulnerability of civilized Faustian western man, his vulnerability to the powers of evil.

Now we have Anthony Burgess's *Earthly Powers*, perhaps the most significant attempt since Mann's *Faustus* to explain recent history in Faustian terms. The novel's original title was *The Affairs of Men*. Then it

From *Modern Fiction Studies* 27, no. 3 (Autumn 1981). © 1981 by the Purdue Research Foundation.

became *The Prince of the Powers of the Air* and finally *Earthly Powers*. The second title was taken from Hobbe's *Leviathan,* part 4, "Of the Kingdom of Darknesse":

> *Besides these Soveraign Powers,* Divine, *and* Humane, *of which I have hitherto discoursed, there is mention in Scripture of another Power, namely, that of the* Rulers of the Darkness of this world, the Kingdome of Satan, *and the* Principality of Beelzebub over Daemons, *that is to say, over Phantasmes that appear in the Air: For which cause Satan is also called* the Prince of the Power of the Air: and (*because he ruleth in the darkness of this world*) The Prince of this world: *And in consequence hereunto, they who are under his Dominion, in opposition to the faithful (who are the* Children of the Light) *are called the* Children of Darknesse.

Burgess quotes this passage in full in *Earthly Powers* [New York: Simon and Schuster, 1980, p. 397, all subsequent references to this edition will be given in the text in parenthesis], as it is being read by the narrator-protagonist, Kenneth M. Toomey, on his way to a visit with the other protagonist, Don Carlo Campanati. Toomey reads further in Hobbes concerning

> *a Confederacy of Deceivers, that to obtain dominion over men in this present world, endeavor by dark and erroneous Doctrines to extinguish in them the Light, both by Nature, and of the Gospell: and so to disprepare them for the Kingdome of God to come.*
>
> (*EP,* 397)

At this point there is no explicit linkage of Don Carlo with the Son of the Morning. Indeed Don Carlo has defined himself primarily in terms of his role as a defender of man against the powers of darkness. But a careful reading of the novel as a whole suggests that the nature of his relationship with the Devil is more equivocal.

For our perception of Don Carlo we are dependent upon Toomey, an eighty-one-year-old homosexual novelist-playwright modeled deliberately on W. Somerset Maugham. The ubiquitous references to Maugham himself and the obvious parallels between Toomey's career and Maugham's make the identification virtually explicit. But the reader may still wonder why Burgess chose to narrate his Faustian drama from such a point of view.

To some extent, one may conjecture, he must have been influenced by some of Maugham's ruminations in such works as *The Summing Up, Looking Back,* and *Don Fernando.* In the last-named work, Maugham discusses the psychology of the homosexual in general terms with specific reference to the case of El Greco:

> Now it cannot be denied that the homosexual has a narrower outlook on the world than the normal man. In certain respects the natural responses of the species are denied to him. Some at least of the broad and typical human emotions he can never experience. However subtly he sees life he cannot see it whole. If it were not for the perplexing sonnets I should say that the homosexual can never reach the supreme heights of genius. I cannot now help asking myself whether what I see in El Greco's work of tortured fantasy and sinister strangeness is not due to such a sexual abnormality as this. . . . I should say that a distinctive trait of the homosexual is a lack of deep seriousness over certain things that normal men take seriously. This ranges from an inane flippancy to a sardonic humour. He has a wilfulness that attaches importance to things that most men find trivial and on the other hand regards cynically the subjects which the common opinion of mankind had held essential to its spiritual welfare. He has a lively sense of beauty, but is apt to see beauty especially in decoration. He loves luxury and attaches peculiar value to elegance. He is emotional, but fantastic. He is vain, loquacious, witty and theatrical. With his keen insight and quick sensibility he can pierce the depths, but in his innate frivolity he fetches up from them not a priceless jewel but a tinsel ornament. He has small power of invention, but a wonderful gift for delightful embroidery. He has vitality, brilliance, but seldom strength. He stands on the bank, aloof and ironical, and watches the river of life flow on.

In some respects, but not in all, this is an accurate picture of Burgess's protagonist. Not being a homosexual himself, Burgess may well have relied upon Maugham's insights into the homosexual psyche. And what seems to have interested him especially were Maugham's remarks upon the ways in which a homosexual artist's vision is limited by his condition. Whether or not Maugham was intentionally drawing in this passage a rather masochistic self-portrait we can only wonder. Certainly he had no illusions about his status as a writer, though he attributed critics' neglect of his work largely to the fact that he had never been a propagandist.

Burgess's protagonist, too, has a sense of his limitations, but he is resentful that the highest honors have gone to others he regards as less deserving:

> As for the Nobel, I did not write inelegantly or tendentiously enough. I was not, like Boris Dyengizhdat, in political chains — which, I felt sure, he would break soon enough when the dollar royalties had mounted sufficiently. I did not, like Chaim Manor or J. Raha Jaatinen, belong to a gallant little nation that, possessing no strategical resources, had to be compensated with a great writer. I was, they had always said, cynical, not given to deep feelings or high thoughts. But I still sold well enough.
>
> (*EP*, 19)

Such remarks of course belie his assertion that he is "not at all bitter." What he says about "Boris Dyengizhdat" inevitably reminds one of Burgess's own remarks about Solzhenitsyn, but we should resist the temptation to take this or any of Toomey's other ruminations as expressions of Burgess's own feelings. At times, such as when he is lecturing at an American college on the craft of fiction, we may strongly suspect that he is speaking for Burgess. But his rather condescending attitude toward Joyce, whom he meets in Paris, hardly resembles Burgess's view of Joyce, and with regard to the crucial issues of the novel, such as the question of human freedom, he is clearly expressing his own point of view, a point of view shaped and limited by his sexual makeup, his Catholic upbringing, and his observations of human experience.

One gathers that Toomey would agree with Maugham when, in the conclusion to *The Summing Up*, he offers an answer to the question: "When then is right action?" His answer is an aphorism of the sixteenth-century Spanish theologian, poet, and teacher Fray Luis de Léon: "The beauty of life is this: it is incumbent upon every man to act according to his nature and his occupation." For Toomey, however, such a saying would have a somewhat different meaning than it probaly had for Fray Luis and, perhaps, for Maugham. Toomey has throughout his long life acted in accord with his nature and his occupation as a writer. Where it has gotten him is clearly revealed in what he himself calls the novel's "*arresting opening*": "It was the afternoon of my eighty-first birthday, and I was in bed with my catamite when Ali announced that the archbishop had come to see me" (*EP*, 7).

Especially suggestive in this first sentence is the word "catamite," evoking as it does an image of refined decadence and pagan luxury in a quasi-Olympian setting. Generally acknowledged "greatness" as a writer has eluded Toomey, but he has achieved a kind of Olympian eminence of fame, wealth, and the freedom of fleshly indulgence that goes with wealth. The Ganymede (L. *Catamitus* altered [*Ganymedes*] Gr. *Ganymedes*, Ganymede) he keeps, however, is no downy-chinned little Greek boy but a fat, sadistic drunkard of a man named Geoffrey Enright, who may be modeled on Gerald Haxton, one of Maugham's secretary-companions. As we soon see, the freedom of fleshly indulgence is also the bondage. Enright is only one of a line of lovers who have made Toomey pay for their favors with more than money. To escape the pain of loneliness, he has had to endure repeatedly humiliation, spite, and treachery.

The fact that Toomey's pederastic play is interrupted by a visit from an archbishop is also significant, foreshadowing much that is to come in the novel. Religion has always gotten in the way of Toomey's pleasures to some extent. Unlike Maugham, he is burdened with a Roman Catholic conscience. As a young man he had felt compelled to leave the Church because he could not refrain from homosexual activity, yet he was convinced that it would damn him, and he had no doubts whatever about the reality of Hell. Unable to reconcile the notion of a God making him as he is, yet forbidding him to act according to his nature, he was driven toward dualism: "But, since God had made me homosexual, I had to believe that there was another God forbidding me to be so. I may say also that I had to believe there were two Christs—one the implacable judge of the Sistine fresco, the other the mild-eyed friend of the disciple John" (*EP*, 52). Later, this dualism develops into a kind of Manichaeism. But heterodoxy cannot save Toomey from his Catholic conscience. Even when he is trying to justify pederasty in an outrageous rewriting of the Book of Genesis, the result, in the words of Ford Madox Ford, "smells of unfrocked priests" (*EP*, 171).

Catholic guilt and the attractions of Manichaeism are familiar themes to Burgess's readers, especially of such novels as *The Worm and the Ring* and *Tremor of Intent*. What is interesting in this new novel is how he relates them to larger themes, sometimes in rather subtle and provocative ways. For instance, when Toomey is setting up the frame story for his rewriting of the Book of Genesis and he is depicting transports of homosexual passion with a lyrical relish and vitality that James Baldwin might envy, he inserts a classical fragment that gives the attentive reader a perspective of the scene and the fable in relation to what the novel as a whole is saying about the human condition and the problem of evil in the modern world. In the frame story, a youngster who is in the process of being fellated by his lover moans out the words *"Solitam . . . Minotauro . . . pro caris corpus,"* words which his lover supposes are "the memory of some old lesson, of some ancient attempt at seduction in that Jesuit school library he had spoken of" (*EP,* 166). Earlier in the novel, and much later in his life, Toomey is watching over his sleeping catamite Geoffrey and is amazed to hear him snore out the same words. Along with the Latin fragment, Geoffrey emits "a ghastly odor . . . of gross decay" that is somehow "remotely familiar" to Toomey. The sleeper becomes for him an image of the human condition, and this prompts a somewhat Augustinian reflection: "Man does not ask for nightmares, he does not ask to be bad. He does not will his own willfulness" (*EP,* 38).

The Latin fragment is from Catullus LXIV, a poem describing the wedding of Thetis and Peleus, on whose marriage bed is a coverlet decorated with pictures of various heroes, including Theseus. The lines in which the words occur are as follows:

> electos iuvenes simul et decus innuptarum
> Cecropiam solitam esse dapem dare Minotauro.
> quis angusta malis cum moenia vexarentur,
> ipse suum Theseus pro caris corpus Athenis
> proicere optavit potius quam talia Cretam
> funera Cecropiae nec funera portarentur.

> Cecropia was wont to give as a feast to the Minotaur chosen youths, and with them the flower of unwedded maids. Now when his narrow walls were troubled by these evils, Theseus himself for his dear Athens chose to offer his own body, rather than that such deaths, living deaths, of Cecropia should be borne to Crete.

In other Burgess novels, notably *The Worm and the Ring* and *Inside Mr. Enderby,* the Minotaur is described as a Greek mythic analogue of Original Sin, and Theseus is seen to be analogous to the heretic Pelagius, who denied Original Sin and asserted that man was capable of achieving perfection without the aid of divine grace. The poet Enderby's *magnum opus* is a long allegorical piece about the Minotaur and about how the labyrinth houses not only the monster but Cretan culture itself " – university, museum, library, art gallery; a treasury of human achievement;

beauty and knowledge built round a core of sin, the human condition."
Then Theseus, who is characterized as "the Pelagian liberator, the man
who had never known sin, the guilt-killer," enters the labyrinth and leads
out the monster on a string. Humanity then seizes the monster, reviles,
buffets, and crucifies it, whereupon the labyrinth collapses, burying
Cretan culture. The poem's argument, as Enderby's homosexual fellow
poet Rawcliffe sums it up, is "Without Original Sin there is no civilization."

The reader of *Earthly Powers,* even if he happens to be familiar with
the works of Catullus and Enderby, may feel that this is a rather overly
subtle way of introducing the Pelagian versus Augustinian theme that
becomes a central concern of the novel, as it is of so many of Burgess's
others. Why must we take such a roundabout and difficult detour through
Catullus? The answer is, I believe, in what Catullus's poem contains
besides the reference to the Minotaur. It relates how the wedding of
Achilles' parents was an event attended by the Olympian gods, who were
wont in days of yore, before religion was despised, to visit the homes of
heroes. Since that time, men and women have sunk to such a level of
depravity, are guilty of so many unnatural sins, including fratricide and
incest, that the gods will no longer visit them. The poem is also about the
betrayal of love, containing, in its description of the abandoned Ariadne
and her lament, one of the most moving passages in Latin poetry. Her
lover-betrayer is also guilty, by reason of his thoughtlessness, of his own
father's death. As the poet presents these betrayals, they completely overshadow the hero's achievement in overcoming the monster.

I am suggesting that Burgess includes this repeated fragmentary
reference to Catullus LXIV because it effectively mirrors the main
thematic concerns of his novel. And he places it in contexts which further
emphasize the same themes. In the first that Toomey happens to recall,
his sleeping catamite, who has just spent an evening humiliating him and
causing him to have a heart attack, becomes a mirror of the fallen human
condition — depraved and vicious but pathetic in his helplessness, in need
of sustaining love human and divine. In the second, Toomey is introducing his revision of the biblical description of the consequences of the fall,
according to which man was deprived of his prelapsarian condition of
homosexual bliss and cursed with the burden of heterosexuality. Those
who are "blessed" with a homosexual nature are able to "remake in their
lives the innocence of Adam ... and their embraces call back the joys of
Eden" (*EP,* 170). Just how little of this Toomey himself really believes is
shown in the scene of cruel, bestial buggery he writes to close his frame

story in this work, which he entitles *A Way Back to Eden*. There is no escaping guilt if one is to remain human. Indeed one who seeks to escape it is likely to become less than human. Man is capable of heroic activity, of overcoming monsters, but until he learns to love and not merely to gratify his appetites in the name of love, he will be overcome by the monsters within him.

That there are monsters abiding within the labyrinth of the human soul is something both Toomey and Don Carlo believe. For Toomey, one of Burgess's "Augustinians," the monsters are the forms of badness that are part of fallen human nature. His own personal monster is his homosexual nature, which he has managed to overcome only once, through the experience of a love that is utterly unlike anything he has ever felt and called by that name. While sojourning in Malaya as a young man, he meets another young man, Doctor Philip Shawcross, whom he soon learns to love, and he recalls how he "marveled at the mystery of a particular nonphysical love apparently driving out generalized physical desire" (*EP*, 242). His love for this man, which is as inexplicable and mysterious as the operation of grace itself, is potentially an avenue of regeneration:

> There was nothing remarkable in Philip's body or brain; I had to resurrect and dust off a concept long discarded by the humanists whom I believed I had joined, namely the *spiritus* of the theologians, the entity you could define only negatively and yet love positively, more, love ardently, with and to the final fire. So, however reluctantly, a man may be brought back to God. There is no free will, we must accept, with love, the imposed pattern.
>
> (*EP*, 243).

The death of this man, which is the result of diabolical machinations, in effect deprives Toomey of a grace bearer, indeed the only source of grace in his life, leaving him prey to the monster of his own nature and the monstrous relationships his nature demands.

For Don Carlo, on the other hand, the monsters within are all intruders who have come from the kingdom of darkness. Because man is God's creation, he is perfect. Evil is wholly from the devil, who taught man how to be evil and is still teaching him. God permits this because He will in no way abridge human freedom. Don Carlo even goes so far as to assert that God, "in His terrible love, denied Himself foreknowledge, imposed upon Himself a kind of human ignorance" of man's fall in Eden, which, if he had foreknown it, would have been predestined, "and where there is predestination there is no freedom of will" (*EP*, 149). Man is still totally free to choose, and his choice is a clear one "between the kingdom of good and the kingdom of evil." Moreover, he has the capacity to negate the consequences of the fall: "God made man without flaw, but also free to become flawed. Yet the flaws are reversible, the return to perfection is possible" (*EP*, 151). Mankind has only one enemy, the enemy of mankind's Creator.

It is these beliefs that shape Carlo's theology and his career. Toomey emphasizes and reemphasizes their importance in his thinking. Initially, they lead him into prominence in the field of exorcism, an activity which Toomey regards as "a lot of nonsense," until he sees Carlo in action in Malaya, in combat with the devils who have been summoned to destroy his friend Doctor Shawcross. A short time later, Toomey sees him in action again, this time in Chicago, attempting the formidable task of exorcizing a bunch of Italian mobsters who have murdered his brother Raffaele. It is the Prohibition era, and in Carlo's view such evils simply demonstrate that "This country has gotten the devil in it" (*EP*, 272). Wherever the devil is at work, it seems, he may expect to encounter Carlo.

While Carlo sees himself as Satan's enemy and a champion of mankind against the powers of darkness, it is suggested early in the novel that he is himself vulnerable to these same powers, and the reader must be attentive to these suggestions if he is to accept some of the later developments in the novel as plausible. The geniunely heretical nature of Carlo's beliefs in human perfectibility is first suggested to Toomey by Carlo's adoptive mother, Concetta Companati:

> "I think what Carlo believes may not be quite orthodox. But orthodoxy may be a matter of strength of will. Carlo thinks you can will anything. Oh, with a bit of grace and prayer as side dishes."
>
> (*EP*, 278)

She has casually but accurately defined him as a Pelagian heretic. A short time later, Carlo himself says to Toomey, "I have never known the impossible to be much trouble. You start off with the impossible, and that is a blank sheet on which the possible may be written" (*EP*, 314). This rather Faustian statement is uttered as he is trying to persuade Toomey to publish under his own name a book setting forth his plans to bring about a reunification of the Christian churches. Essential to the achievement of this end are drastic alterations in orthodox Catholic doctrines with regard to the role of the Pope, the Real Presence in the Eucharist, and other matters.

The liturgy of the mass, he argues, should be malleable enough to be altered in harmony with local customs and cultural traditions, and the example he gives of how this might work, which becomes important later in the novel, is the African mass, in which dancing and chanting would replace "the imposition of organ voluntaries or Western hymns." "Here," as Toomey describes it, "was the terrible ecumenical strategy set out in clumsy single-spaced typing, and I, who considerd myself to have lost my faith, was appalled" (*EP,* 316).

Predictably, the treatise goes on to argue in defense of Pelagius himself and for acceptance of his teachings, "as more consonant with the True Reformed premise of the goodness and dignity of man than the Augustinian doctrine of his natural depravity" (*EP,* 319). What especially worries Toomey, who, largely because of his own nature and experience, inclines toward Augustinianism, is the virtual absence of any discussion of sin, Original or other:

> Dangerous this denial of original sin, though it was not expressed in so many words. You could blame yourself for lack of moral judgement, but not for the dynamic which animated your acts of evil. Original sin was original weakness, not being sufficiently clever, or Godlike, to spot the machinations of the fiend.
>
> (*EP,* 318)

At this point, the reader will perceive, if he has not already perceived, that the model for Carlo is Pope John XXIII, the most beloved pontiff of modern times. As with the characterization of Toomey, Burgess has made the character larger and, in some ways, more heroic than the model. But he has also, as with the characterization of Toomey, made him a good deal less attractive than his model. Eventually he develops into a very sinister figure indeed, one who seems to have acquired his earthly powers by means of a Faustian bargain. Why, we may wonder, does Burgess do this? Why diminish John XXIII? The answer, I believe, is in the passages I have just quoted. Burgess is not diminishing Pope John himself so much as what he and his ecumenicism seemed to represent, a revival of the Pelagian heresy and a willingness to achieve the reunification of Christianity at the cost of abandoning the very essence of Catholicism. Pelagianism is an attractive heresy, but, as Burgess suggests in the secular contexts of *The Wanting Seed* and *A Clockwork Orange,* it inevitably breeds "DISAPPOINTMENT," which in turn causes people to become extremely Augustinian in their thinking, which in turn may lead to evil consequences. Pope John XXIII, he seems to be suggesting, may have set in motion processes which his successors might not be able to control.

Whether or not Burgess is correct in his thinking about John XXIII is a question to be discussed outside the context of a critical exegesis of *Earthly Powers*. Personally I think he is wrong, but that does not prevent me from appreciating his Faustian characterization, which is both reminiscent of other great Faustian protagonists and highly original. He is indeed a much more absorbing character than Toomey, who tends to become rather wearisome after a while. We see so much of Toomey, too much of him. His sexual problems and humiliations arouse sympathy but also disgust, and this, I suspect, will be the reaction of any reader, no matter what his or her sexual makeup happens to be. His preoccupation with his own importance, or lack of it, as a writer is also wearing. Carlo, on the other hand, is a richly developed character whom we can visualize clearly but who retains elements of mystery which stimulate and free the reader's imagination.

A crucial event in Carlo's development is the discovery that he is adopted. This has been foreshadowed in a kind of epiphany Toomy experiences as he compares Carlo physically with the other Companatis: "Carlos was physically gross in comparison with that pared and elegant family. In a flash I saw him as a changeling, a goblin baby dumped in a Campanati pram" (*EP*, 156). The passage is worth quoting because it in effect suggests the possibility of enchanted, even demonic origins. As it happens, Carlo finds out that he can never be certain about his origins, and the effect of this on him is initally devastating. In the process of coming to terms with this fact, with the anesthetizing aid of strong drink, he is prompted to engage in what turns out to be a conjuring. By means of cursing and blasphemy, he succeeds in summoning either the devil himself or a phantasm of him in the form of a large rat, "whose sleek fur and bright teeth Carlo admired extravagantly in various languages, including, I think, Aramaic" (*EP*, 332). What follows is a kind of monologue-dialogue with the devil, reminiscent of the demonic dialogues of Adrian Leverkühn and Ivan Karamazov. Wisely, Burgess does not try to imitate these celebrated dialogues, even as Virgil wisely eschews imitating certain episodes in Homer that cannot be surpassed. What he gives us, however, is powerfully evocative:

> In the tones of an upper-class Englishman he said, "For the moment you are in the ascendancy, old boy, what, rather. I see your large clean fangs grinning at my temporary failure. *Salut,*

mon prince, votre bloody *altesse*. You and I are alike in not possessing a mater, old boy. Even God forced himself into a filial situation. But will prevails, don't you know. There is never any failure of the will. We are what we make ourselves, old chap. Let's see you now as a serpent, your first disguise. Very good, that's really a most remarkable cobra hood, old fellow. I've never been much afraid of snakes, don't you know. The colonial experience, so to say, *mon brave*. But you bore me rather, you tire me somewhat. A little shut-eye is indicated, wouldn't you say? Rather."

                                        (*EP*, 332)

Significantly, Toomey reports this without any skeptical comment, though he himself has not actually seen the apparition, except through Carlo's eyes.

Having overcome the shock of discovering that his parentage is unknown, Carlo apparently undergoes some changes in personality, and the reader can only infer that his meeting with the devil, whether real or imagined, has had something to do with these changes. He now despises the family that had adopted him, regarding them all as "failures," whose only admirable qualities can be accounted for in terms of weaknesses or folly. Though he professes to be "brimming" with compassion, we can see that a hardness and a coldness have set in and along with these qualities a growth in pride and ambition. He reveals to Toomey his intention to "make Pope." No longer despondent about his mysterious origins, he likens himself to Oedipus, a "son of the goddess Fortune," who is free to make what he will of her gifts to him. Above all, he intends to "survive," like the Church itself, all the ephemeral forces of destruction in the modern world. Neither he nor the Church will be what he calls contemptuously a "victim."

Actually, he has more in common with Oedipus than he realizes. His contempt for victims and failures and his complete confidence in himself manifest what Toomey rightly suggests is an attitude bordering on *hubris*. Much later, after he has learned humility from perhaps the only one who can teach him, Carlo recalls his earlier conversation with Toomey about Oedipus and Greek tragedy. Having been shown by the devil himself, during an abortive exorcism, the limits of his powers, he admits in effect that he has been guilty of *hubris*. What he does not realize is that he, like Oedipus, is a man whose illusions of freedom and power will blind him as he is caught up in the process of fulfilling a strange, terrible fate. The devil sees to it that he will remain blinded. As he is in the process of casually breaking the neck of the possessed victim, he hails Carlo as "*Sancte Pater.*"

Before Carlo's humiliation by the devil, which appears to be instrumental in leading him to make a Faustian pact whereby he becomes indeed *Sancte Pater,* Carlo is able to maintain the illusion of his own power against the forces of evil. And his Pelagian belief in the essential goodness and perfectibility of man does not abandon him, even when it is tested by spectacles of the Nazis in action. During the Nazi occupation in Italy, he, as Bishop of Moneta, becomes a heroic figure in the resistance movement, and when an SS officer named, significantly, Liebeneiner, falls into his hands, he reassumes his old role of exorcist and undertakes the formidable task of driving out the devil Hitler. Eventually, through force and persistence, he succeeds, at least to the extent of disillusioning the man and removing his former beliefs. But the whole effort, albeit finally crowned with a degree of success, reveals that the root of the problem is an evil that does not come from the Kingdom of Darkness outside of man.

The episode of Liebeneiner's conversion, one of the most memorable passages in the novel, effectively illuminates the limitations of Carlo's understanding imposed by his Pelagian view of human nature. The man is, Carlo believes, "a new type of human being" produced by Nazi Germany, one who is "capable of putting the abstraction of a political system before the realities of human life" and willing, when ordered, "to perpetuate the most ghastly enormities without remorse" (*EP,* 416). Carlo's explanation for this, as for all human evil, is that "The devil got into" Liebeneiner and his people. In Liebeneiner's particular case, there was "a kind of vacuum" to begin with, and the process of saving his soul is made different for Carlo by the fact that it is "not much of a soul." What Carlo does not grasp is that Liebeneiner is not merely a representative Nazi but a representative of the fallen human condition in the modern age—fragmented, capable of utterly separating his sense of duty from his humanity, in desperate need of grace secular or divine. He is indeed a "vacuum," a living embodiment of the privative concept of evil, revealing, like Shakespeare's Iago, an essential emptiness. As his very name indicates, he is without love, and this is the vacuum the Nazis have filled with devotion to the German state. Carlo in effect imposes irresistible grace upon him and forcibly achieves his regeneration.

Immediately following this episode in the novel, and in effect juxtaposed with it, is Toomey's own view of the same triumph of evil. He relates how he was sent, at the end of the war, with a parliamentary delegation to

visit Buchenwald. Viewing the horrors, he, like Carlo discovering Liebeneiner's inhumanity, thinks first of "The Prince of the Power of the Air,"
but then he quickly rejects this explanation: "No. This was no Luciferian
work. The intellectual rebel against God could not stoop to it. This was
pure man, pure me" (EP, 426). His revulsion and disgust carry him
beyond even Augustinian pessimism: "Man had not been tainted from
without by the Prince of the Power of the Air. The evil was all in him and
he was beyond hope of redemption" (EP, 427). He does not, like Carlo,
believe that the Nazis had produced "a new type of human being." Indeed, in his view, they had produced nothing essentially new but had
merely exploited on a vast scale the evil that men have always found
within themselves:

> The Nazis had, in a quantitative age, exploited the horror of
> surfeit: that was their sole new achievement . . . I wanted to
> have Carlo with me there to smell the ripe Gorgonzola of in-
> nate human evil and to dare to say that mankind was God's
> creation and hence good. Good, that's what I am, sir, it was
> the devil made me do it. Man was not God's creation, that was
> certain. God alone knew from what suppurating primordial
> dungheap man had arisen."
>
> (EP, 427)

As he recalls this bitter meditation, Toomey relates how he had
discovered a scrap of paper clinging to his foot. On it was the same Latin
fragment: "Solitam . . . Minotauro . . . pro caris corpus." It is never
explicitly identified in the novel, but to the reader who recognizes it in
context it becomes progressively more meaningful. We are being led in
effect ever further into the labyrinth of the human soul, and the monsters
are becoming ever more threatening.

By juxtaposing Carlo's and Toomey's contradictory views and explanations of the Nazis, Burgess does not seem to be suggesting that one
or the other is wholly correct. He suggests rather that both views are to
some extent partially correct, but both are also significantly limited.
Viewing the spectacle of twentieth-century history, Toomey would at-
tribute the triumphs of evil wholly to innate human depravity, while
Carlo would credit them wholly to the devil. In fact, as Burgess's depiction of events suggests, there is an interaction, a cooperation between the
demons that are a part of man's nature and the devil himself. Failure to
recognize the existence of both may lead to dreadful consequences.

The demons within Carlo which lead him in effect to become the instrument of his enemy are pride and ambition, the very demons that led man into the fallen condition Carlo refuses to recognize. His Faustian pact with the devil is never actually shown in the novel. Indeed it may not be *consciously* made, but it is strongly suggested, nonetheless, by the events that follow his ascendancy to the papal chair which was linked to his reign. He does indeed "make Pope," becoming a beloved pontiff who is recognized as a champion of mankind against the devils of social injustice. He also initiates changes that threaten to transform the Church beyond recognition. When he dies, he becomes a candidate for sainthood.

Crucial to Carlo's canonization is the verification of a miracle attributed to him, and it happens that Toomey is the only witness. When the two men had been visiting Carlo's dying brother Raffaele in a Chicago hospital, they had seen a child dying of spinal meningitis, and somehow Carlo, "through the fierce gentle compassion of his presence" (*EP*, 271) had managed to bring about a complete cure. As it turns out, this miracle is ultimately responsible for bringing about one of the most ghastly triumphs of evil in recent history. The child survives to become "God Manning," a fanatical religious leader modeled obviously on the late Jim Jones. Burgess transfers what is obviously Jonestown and the horrible events there from Guyana to the Mojave Desert in California. In linking Carlo with them, Burgess appears to be suggesting that Carlo's role as an instrument of the devil actually began long before he became Pope. While Carlo firmly believes that good can be wrought out of evil, his miracle effectively shows how the powers of darkness are able to use what is essentially good for their own purposes. There is also the suggestion of Carlo's direct connection with other evils, including the destruction of two of the most attractive characters in the novel, who apparently become sacrificial victims in an African mass of the kind Carlo had advocated.

Carlo's Faustian identity is made explicit near the end of the novel, when a priest asks Toomey to tell him what Carlo had said to his, Toomey's, sister when she visited him near the moment of his death. Carlo had professed his love for her, a love like that of Dante for Beatrice. Hearing this, the priest utters the most famous line in Goethe's *Faust* and asks Toomey to quote it in the original: *"Das Ewig-Weibliche zieht uns hinan"* (*EP*, 600). The line doesn't seem to be all that relevant because Toomey's sister has not, like Gretchen in *Faust*, played any vital role in Carlo's Faustian progress, though she may, as the only human being he seems truly to have loved, serve potentially as a grace-bearing agent of his salvation. On the other hand, it may be a bitterly ironic allusion, like the epigraph from *Faust* that introduces Malcolm Lowry's drama of damnation, *Under the Volcano*.

There is a great deal to discuss in *Earthly Powers* besides the Faustian drama of Carlo Campanati. What needs to be discussed in a larger essay than this one is how Burgess integrates all the many parts of this vast and demanding novel. I do not doubt that the connections between Toomey's accounts of social, literary, and political history will be worked on in future critical exegeses. Burgess is clearly in command of his material, and it remains for us to appreciate critically what he has achieved. I tend to agree with those who call it his "masterpiece," though it is certainly not without flaws. Parts of it are, as I have said, wearisome, and the language is occasionally pedantic. The flaws are, however, minor and unavoidable in a work so large and ambitious. Overall it is a magnificent performance, what we have been waiting for from Burgess.

WALTER KERR

The Poet and the Pop Star:
Enderby's Dark Lady

Directly beneath the already doubled title of Anthony Burgess's fourth novel about Enderby, a fat and frequently dislocated minor British poet (Tangier, Rome, New York, Indiana, various time-warps), there is an additional bit of information. The work, Mr. Burgess tells us, was "composed to placate kind readers of 'The Clockwork Testament, or Enderby's End,' who objected to my casually killing my hero."

Personally, I wouldn't have called the catastrophic events that concluded the immediately preceding novel all that casual. Enderby had opened his apartment door in New York City, where he'd been doing a stint of teaching as a result of having been connected with a scandalous film version of Gerard Manley Hopkins's "The Wreck of the Deutschland," to find himself toe to toe with yet another of the gift-women his author so freely bestows on him. (Enderby rarely, if ever, has to work for his women; they acquire him, like poor reputations.)

This one has a gun in her hand and is going to rid herself of the poet and, she hopes, his work. She has, much against her will, become a compulsive reader of Enderby's verse. This cannot continue; she abhors compulsions of any kind. She will therefore devictimize herself by blasting the gentleman to bits, snarling the while. Enderby, who is able enough when it comes to customs inspectors or armed women, successfully disarms her and then either rapes or seduces her. Either would constitute a modest advance for our near-impotent friend. Thereafter he settles

From *The New York Times Book Review* (April 22, 1984). © 1984 by the New York Times Company.

himself down on a pile of pouffes and watches, very much to his surprise, a television film having to do with St. Augustine and the Pelagian Heresy. He is found dead of a heart attack next morning.

What is interesting about Mr. Burgess's willingness to restore his man to life is that he does not bother to do it in the old Universal Pictures way: He doesn't have the monster fall through the floor of the flaming mill into a saving pool of water, or anything ridiculous like that. No. He simply supposes that two opposites can concur at one and the same time, and why not? Of course, no existentialist philosopher would let him do that. Your average exisentialist would point out that the choice of Enderby dead in New York eliminates the choice of Enderby alive in Indiana, and that it is precisely all those eliminated choices that fill modern man with *Angst,* with a sense of living among rejections, above a void.

But Enderby, you see, does not really suffer from *Angst,* nor does Mr. Burgess. Enderby suffers from cholesterol buildup and bad cigars; Mr. Burgess suffers from a fondness for adverbs like "queenlily" and a growing reliance on irrelevant set-pieces. But we must grant the two writers their double-jointed universe, partly because they have so often provided us with savage fun, and partly because we're all headed for science-fiction anyway.

In point of fact, the final chapter of *Enderby's Dark Lady is* sci-fi, and, though it does not feature Enderby because Enderby is its author, it is quite shiveringly written, especially when a space-time visitor to Elizabethan England is struggling to keep the rooms he is passing through from dissolving before he has passed through them.

Considerably less felicitous, I am sorry to say, is an opening stretch in *Jacobean* England that purports to be a short narrative, also imagined by Enderby, detailing Ben Jonson's role in the Gunpowder Plot (spy for the Court) and Shakespeare's contribution to the King James Bible (worked his name into the 46th Psalm). While this particular set-piece does serve to secure Enderby an invitation to a university theater in Indiana (where he will be expected to concoct a musical based on Shakespeare's life, times and dark lady), it is otherwise quite unnecessary. Also, it's not really much better than the standard semischolarly, faintly impertinent stabs at evoking the period that college students have been turning out, and turning in as term papers, for years.

There are other curious collapses of tone. An improvised sermon delivered by an uncomfortable Enderby before a black congregation in North Carolina is simply bewildering, neither amusing nor to any discernible point. And when Enderby, just arrived in Indiana, is attempting to deal with a supercilious stage director (Toplady) and an arrogant if un-tutored composer (Silversmith) at the Peter Brook Theater, Mr. Burgess seems suddenly uncertain of his targets. We're ready for satirical mayhem, remembering all that has happened so hilariously to "The Wreck of the Deutschland" just one book away. And this new novel hints at trouble brewing: "Toplady had done a nude *Macbeth* somewhere. He appeared to have little confidence in Enderby. Enderby reciprocated with all his heartburn."

But shortly Enderby is supposing that Toplady "seemed to know what he wanted" and is obligingly doing foolish rewrites (on what was presumably a foolish script to begin with). But the arrows aren't flying either way — the mild flings at parody seem to cancel each other out. Mr. Burgess appears to have lost real enthusiasm for the cultural battle as he has waged it before.

Until, that is to say, the dark lady herself puts in a delayed ap-pearance. She is a black pop singing star doing a guest stint on campus, she has been on campuses before and can give you noumenon and/or phenomenon at the least whiff of Kant, and, when Kant is not wanted, she can always slip into her "Topsy act." As she says, bestowing her bless-ing on Enderby, "Baby, you may be an uptight ofay milktoast limey bastard, but you ain't no fag." She is good for the poet's self-esteem, and he seriously falls in love with her, as many of Mr. Burgess's readers are apt to do, starting here, starting now.

When I say that Enderby "seriously" falls in love with her, I mean that this aging, rhyme-drunk near-misogynist who was frightened by sex at an early age (and who has been known to abandon the act in mid-light in order to make notes for a sonnet) is forced to define both his ardor and his sexual reluctance ruthlessly. His open declaration of love is filled with an entirely plausible rage. His bitter analysis of the interdependence of love and lust is masterly. We understand him better by the time he's ex-hausted his fury, still preposterous and sad and honest and hopeless, still undecided as to whether he's more nearly Falstaff or Silenus.

He's neither. He's an original, this out-of-sync singer of earnestly obscure melodies, who prefers to write his verse while seated on a toilet and has "always found it difficult to be insincere." And, in this fourth book of Mr. Burgess's Enderbean Apocalypse, it is the dark lady and the dark lady alone who brings him to pitch. (Her professional name is April Elgar. She chose the name Elgar because, as a child, she admired the com-poser of a tune she thought was called Pompous Circus Dance.)

The novel, as novel, is more nearly patchwork than clockwork. And pretty brazen about it, too. But, now that April's here, it can safely be welcomed by all those Burgess fans who simply cannot conceive of a world without Enderby.

Chronology

1917   Born February 25, in Manchester, England. Son of Joseph Wilson, a pianist, and "Beautiful Belle Burgess," a musical comedy actress.

1918   Mother and sister die of influenza.

1940   B.A. in English from Manchester University. Joins British Army Education Corps.

1942   Marries Llewella Isherwood Jones. She suffers a miscarriage.

1946–48 Lecturer at Birmingham University.

1949   Writes *A Vision of Battlements* (not published until 1965), first of 28 novels and many nonfiction books to date.

1950   English Master at Banbury Grammar School.

1954–59 Serves as an education officer in Colonial Service in Malaya and Borneo. Invalided home in 1959, with diagnosed brain tumor (diagnosis proves wrong). Publishes Malayan trilogy: *Time for a Tiger* (1956), *The Enemy in the Blanket* (1958), *Beds in the East* (1959).

1960–63 Publishes *The Right to an Answer, The Doctor Is Sick, The Worm and the Ring, Devil of a State, One Hand Clapping, A Clockwork Orange, The Wanting Seed, Honey for the Bears,* and *Inside Mr. Enderby* (all novels).

1964   Son Andreas born. Publishes *The Eve of Saint Venus* and *Nothing Like the Sun* (novels).

1965–67   *Here Comes Everybody* (criticism), *Tremor of Intent* (novel), and *The Novel Now* (criticism).

1968   First wife dies. Marries Liliana Macellari, and family moves to Malta to avoid taxation. *Enderby Outside* (novel).

1969   Writer-in-Residence at the University of North Carolina.

1970–71   Teaches creative writing at Princeton. Publishes a biography of Shakespeare, and *MF*, a novel. Film version of *A Clockwork Orange*.

1972–73   Visiting Professor at City College, New York City. *Joysprick* (criticism); *Cyrano*, a musical comedy version of Cyrano de Bergerac, for which Burgess does translation and composes the music.

1974   *The Clockwork Testament; or, Enderby's End*, and *Napoleon Symphony* (novels).

1976   *Beard's Roman Women* (novel), *Moses: A Narrative* (narrative poem). Moves to Monaco.

1977–78   *Abba Abba* (novel), *Hemingway and His World* (biography), *1985* (novel).

1979   *Man of Nazareth* (a novel, based on Burgess's screenplay for the television drama "Jesus of Nazareth").

1980   *Earthly Powers* (novel).

1982   *The End of the World News* (novel).

1984   *Enderby's Dark Lady; or, No End to Enderby* (novel).

1985   *The Kingdom of the Wicked* (novel).

1986   *But Do Blondes Prefer Gentlemen?* (collection of essays), *The Pianoplayers* (novel).

1987   *Little Wilson and Big God* (memoirs).

Contributors

HAROLD BLOOM, Sterling Professor of the Humanities at Yale University, is the author of *The Anxiety of Influence, Poetry and Repression*, and many other volumes of literary criticism. A MacArthur Prize Fellow, he is general editor of five series of literary criticism published by Chelsea House.

CHRISTOPHER RICKS, formerly King Edward VII Professor of English Literature at Cambridge University and currently Professor of English at Boston University, is the author of *Milton's Grand Style, Keats and Embarrassment*, among other books, and has edited critical volumes of Tennyson and A. E. Housman. He is a Fellow of the British Academy and is the co-editor of the journal *Essays in Criticism*.

WILLIAM H. PRITCHARD, the author of *Lives of the Modern Poets*, is Professor of English at Amherst College.

ROBERT K. MORRIS is the author of *Paradoxes of Order* and *The Consolations of Ambiguity*.

JOHN J. STINSON teaches in the English Department of the State University of New York at Fredonia.

JEAN E. KENNARD, Professor of English at the University of New Hampshire, is the author of *Number and Nightmare* and *Victims of Convention*.

ESTHER PETIX is a teacher in the public school system in Suffern, New York.

GEOFFREY AGGELER is Professor of English at the University of Utah, Salt Lake City, and is the author of *Anthony Burgess: The Artist as Novelist*.

TIMOTHY R. LUCAS is a freelance writer who lives in Cincinnati.

WALTER KERR, retired drama critic of *The New York Times* and winner of the Pulitzer Prize, is the author of *The Decline of Pleasure* and *The Silent Clowns*.

Bibliography

Aggeler, Geoffrey, *Anthony Burgess: The Artist as Novelist*. University: University of Alabama Press, 1979
——. "Between God and Not God: Anthony Burgess' *Tremor of Intent*." *Malahat Review*, no. 17 (1971): 90–102.
——. "The Comic Art of Anthony Burgess." *Arizona Quarterly* 25, no. 3 (1969): 234–51.
——. "Mr. Enderby and Mr. Burgess." *Malahat Review*, no. 10 (1969): 104–10.
——. "A Wagnerian Affirmation: The Worm and the Ring." *Western Humanities Review* 27, no. 4 (1973): 401–10.
Brophy, Elizabeth. "*A Clockwork Orange:* English and Nadsat." *Notes on Contemporary Literature* 2, no. 2 (1972): 4–6.
Chalpin, L. "Anthony Burgess, Gallows Humor in Dystopia." *Texas Quarterly* 16 (1973): 227–30.
Chew, Shirley. "Mr. Livedog's Day: The Novels of Anthony Burgess." *Encounter* 38, no. 6 (1972): 57–64.
Clemons, Walter. "Anthony Burgess: Pushing On." *New York Times Book Review* (November 29, 1972), 2.
Coale, Samuel. *Anthony Burgess*. New York: Ungar, 1981.
Connelly, Wayne C. "Optimism in Burgess' *A Clockwork Orange*." *Extrapolation: A Science Fiction Newsletter* 14, no. 1 (1972): 25–59.
Cullinan, John. "Burgess' *The Wanting Seed*." *Explicator* 31, no. 7 (March 1973): item 51.
Dix, Carol. *Anthony Burgess*. London: Longman, 1971.
——. "Anthony Burgess." *Transatlantic Review* 42/43, no. 2 (1972): 62–66.
Duffy, Charles F. "From Espionage to Eschatology: Anthony Burgess' *Tremor of Intent*." *Renascence* 32 (1980): 79–88.
Evans, Robert O. "Nadsat: The Argot and Its Implications in Anthony Burgess' *A Clockwork Orange*." *Journal of Modern Literature* 1, no. 3 (1971): 406–10.
Friedman, Melvin J. "Anthony Burgess and James Joyce: A Literary Confrontation." *Literary Criterion* 9, no. 4 (1971): 71–83.
Isaacs, Neil D. "Unstuck in Time: *A Clockwork Orange* and *Slaughterhouse Five*." *Literature/Film Quarterly* 1, no. 2 (1973): 122–31.
Kennard, Jean. "*MF:* A Separable Meaning." *Riverside Quarterly* 6 (1975): 200–206.

LeClair, Thomas. "Essential Opposition: The Novels of Anthony Burgess." *Critique* 12, no. 3 (1971): 77–94.

Mathews, Richard. *The Clockwork Orange Universe of Anthony Burgess*. Popular Writers of Today, no. 19. San Bernadino, Calif.: Borgo, 1978.

Mitchell, Julian. "Anthony Burgess." *London Magazine* 3, no. 11 (1964): 48–54.

Modern Fiction Studies 27, no. 3 (Autumn 1981). Special Anthony Burgess issue.

Mowat, John. "Joyce's Contemporary: A Study of Anthony Burgess' *Napoleon Symphony*." *Contemporary Literature* 19 (1978): 180–95.

Page, Malcolm. "Anthony Burgess: The Artist as Performer." *West Coast Review* 4, no. 3 (1970): 21–24.

Palumbo, Ronald J. "Names and Games in *Tremor of Intent*." *English Language Notes* 18 (1980): 48–51.

Rabinovitz, Rubin. "Ethical Values in Anthony Burgess's *A Clockwork Orange*." *Studies in the Novel* 11, no. 1 (1979): 43–50.

Stinson, John J. "Anthony Burgess: Novelist on the Margin." *Journal of Popular Culture* 7, no. 1 (1973): 136–51.

Wood, Michael. "A Dream of Clockwork Oranges." *New Society* (June 6, 1968), 842–43.

Zaehner, Robert C. "Rot in the Clockwork Orange." In *Our Savage God: The Perverse Use of Eastern Thought*, 19–73. New York: Sheed & Ward, 1974.

Acknowlegments

"The Epicene" by Christopher Ricks from *The New Statesman* 65, no. 1673 (April 5, 1963), ©1963 by The Statesman and Nation Publishing Co., Ltd. Reprinted by permission.

"The Novels of Anthony Burgess" by William H. Pritchard from *The Massachusetts Review* 3, no. 3 (Summer 1966), ©1966 by The Massachusetts Review, Inc. Reprinted by permission.

"Mr. Kell and Mr. Burgess: Inside and Outside Mr. Enderby" by Charles G. Hoffman and A. C. Hoffmann from *The Shaken Realist: Essays in Modern Literature in Honor of Frederick J. Hoffmann,* edited by Melvin J. Friedman and John B. Vickery, ©1970 by Louisiana State University Press. Reprinted by permission.

"The Bitter Fruits of Freedom" by Robert K. Morris from *The Consolations of Ambiguity: An Essay on the Novels of Anthony Burgess* by Robert K. Morris, ©1971 by the Curators of the University of Missouri. Reprinted by permission of the University of Missouri Press.

"The Manichee World of Anthony Burgess" by John J. Stinson from *Renascence* 26, no. 1 (Autumn 1973), ©1973 by the Catholic Renascence Society, Inc. Reprinted by permission.

"Anthony Burgess: Double Vision" by Jean E. Kennard from *Number and Nightmare: Forms of Fantasy in Contemporary Fiction* by Jean E. Kennard, ©1975 by Archon Books, The Shoestring Press, Inc. Reprinted by permission.

"Linguistics, Mechanics, and Metaphysics: *A Clockwork Orange*" (originally entitled "Linguistics, Mechanics, and Metaphysics: Anthony Burgess's *A Clockwork Orange* [1962]") by Esther Petix from *Old Lines, New Forces: Essays on the Contemporary British Novel, 1960–1970,* edited by Robert K. Morris, ©1976 by Associated University Presses, Inc. Reprinted by permission.

"Joycean Burgess" (originally entitled "Counterparts") by Robert Martin Adams from *Afterjoyce: Studies in Fiction after Joyce* by Robert Martin Adams, ©1977 by Robert Martin Adams. Reprinted by permission of Oxford University Press.

"Pelagius and Augustine" by Geoffrey Aggeler from *Anthony Burgess: The Artist as Novelist* by Geoffrey Aggeler, ©1979 by the University of Alabama Press. Reprinted by permission.

"The Old Shelley Game: Prometheus and Predestination in Burgess's Works" by Timothy R. Lucas from *Modern Fiction Studies* 27, no. 3 (Autumn 1981), ©1981 by the Purdue Research Foundation. Reprinted by permission of the Purdue Research Foundation, West Lafayette, Indiana.

"Faust in the Labyrinth: *Earthly Powers*" (originally entitled "Faust in the Labyrinth: Burgess' *Earthly Powers*") by Geoffrey Aggeler from *Modern Fiction Studies* 27, no. 3 (Autumn 1981), ©1981 by the Purdue Research Foundation. Reprinted by permission of the Purdue Research Foundation, West Lafayette, Indiana.

"The Poet and the Pop Star: *Enderby's Dark Lady*" (originally entitled "The Poet and the Pop Star") by Walter Kerr from *The New York Times Book Review* (April 22, 1984), ©1984 by the New York Times Company. Reprinted by permission.

Index